I have endured, I have been broken, I have known hardship. I have lost myself. But here I stand, still moving forward, growing stronger each day. I will never forget the harsh lessons in my life. They made me stronger.

Morgan Rees

Endurance is Victory

ISBN: 979-8-218-16448-5 (Paperback)

Portions of this book are works of nonfiction. Certain names and identifying characteristics have been changed to protect the identities of those involved.

Front cover image by Morgan Rees.
Book design by Morgan Rees.

Printed by Ingram Spark, Inc., in the United States of America.

First printing edition 2020.

Morgan Rees
P.O. Box 690304
Charlotte, NC, 28227

https://www.morganreesauthor1.com/

AUTHOR'S BIOGRAPHY

First, I would like to thank God for giving me the strength and courage after all these years, I could finally come out and tell my story. For a long time, I feared anyone knowing what type of life I lived. Second, this is the first book I have ever written, but I could pull it off with the help of the Lord and the sincere support from my family and friends, who knew more of my life. However, my major influence for writing my story was to tell people about my life and give them some hope. No matter what type of life you live, experiences should strengthen you, not weaken you, especially because you are a survivor and warrior, never a victim.

In addition, you can endure anything in life without the overuse of drugs, alcohol, doing something illegal, or something that may violate you more. Honestly, I can say that I am a true testament to that. Last, I would like to thank my ex-mother-in-law, for helping me come up with the title and giving me the confidence to complete this book. I

Endurance is Victory

was born in Brooklyn, New York, but I lived in Philadelphia, Pennsylvania all my life until the year 2004, when I moved to Augusta, Georgia, and now, I am in my forever home and new life in Charlotte, NC. I grew up as a person who always had to prove myself to my family or get approval from friends and people for acceptance. I have struggled all of my life in order to give my children a better life than I had, I never had much when I was a child, and I never received the love that I believe I should have received, so I tried my best to make sure that my children did not go through the same thing.

However, today I can happily say that I can show my children, grandchildren, and everyone that you can overcome any obstacles, roadblocks, boulders, and walls placed in your life if you persevere, and never give up no matter the circumstance. For the first time in over 26- years, I am the happiest I have ever been. I have found peace, joy, and stability that I could never accomplish during the past chapters of my life, until I chose not to give up the fight, and not let my past life define who I am, my outcome, and the goals that I am going to achieve on my new journey of life.

ENDURANCE IS VICTORY

My name is Katrina; I was born on September 9, 1973, in Brooklyn, New York, in King County Hospital. My mother, Leslie, was in labor on Labor Day, the day I was born. I lived in New York from the time of birth until the age of 5-years-old. From what I could remember, and then, my mother moved to Darlington, South Carolina, a little town, about an hour from Fayetteville, North Carolina.

From that time, I can remember that my life has been full of chaos, pain, disappointment, hurt, confusion, frustration, and being misunderstood. I was born with a skin condition called; "Eczema," which caused me to have very low self-esteem and I lacked confidence in myself, but the more you read about my life, you will see why. And now, here is the story of my life!

As far as I can remember, I always felt treated like an outsider by my mother, my family, and some of my so-called friends. All the feelings of neglect started with my mother, grandmother, and down to some of my aunts and cousins on my maternal side of the family. From

Endurance is Victory

life experiences and life teachings, I was always told that, if you cannot get love and respect from anyone else, you could always run home to your mother, because she will always be there for you, stand by your side, and always have your back, no matter what the situation is. Well, in my case, that was not the situation, every time I ran to my mother, she would always push me away with either harsh words or always chastising me even when I was not disobedient. So, from that time, until I became an adult, I just dealt with the card's life dealt to me.

As a young child, I was always being teased and taunted about my skin and my clothes by children my age or older, and sometimes even adults. In addition, when I would go to my mother for comfort and understanding, or even words of encouragement, she would always push me away or even at times agree with them. Then, I would run to other family members and they would do the same or tease me, making matters even worse. Except for one person in my family and that person was my mother's second older sister, Tracy, and her children for that time being, especially her oldest child, Iesha, who was a year older than me. That was the only time I had a little happiness when they would come to visit, even though they would sometimes treat me the same as the rest of the family.

However, they would be the only people that would not mind being around me because of my skin condition and would always be there for me and defend me when other children would tease me or want to get into fights with me for being too smart or ugly. I can also remember the times when Aunt Tracy and her kids would spend the night over at our house and we would play school and other child-like games.

These times would be the only times that my mom would allow me to be myself and not fuss and complain about me or every little thing and I felt like I had a little freedom. But sometimes I would get whippings for something and my mom would sometimes call my Aunt Tracy over to whip me because either she did not feel like doing it or she would have rather for my aunt to do it for her. See, back in those times, adults valued the saying, "It takes a village to raise a child," and they lived by it because not just your mother would chastise you, it could have been anyone, your next-door neighbor, a new friend, your grandmother or even a distant relative.

Endurance is Victory

In my case, it was mostly my Aunt Tracy or my mother. Some of my mother other brothers and sisters would always taunt me by giving me nicknames like rat, alligator, scaly, Diggy mo (because I scratched a lot), and sometimes, if we had different family functions, I could not always go because of their embarrassment of me. I would curse the family because of my looks. In addition, what would make me so mad and feel very hurt, was making me feel as if my family did not want me, especially my mother most of those times.

I can remember with my mother's family, there was this one occasion where we were sitting around my grandmother's house and as usual, the conversation stemmed around my looks. I had an Aunt Sarah, who was a makeup freak and she always had this bright idea that maybe covering up my face with makeup would make me look better, at least better than I already was. Well, the sad thing with the make-up was that I was allergic to it. I told them this, and I still let her put the make-up on my face anyway. Of course, you know what happened, my skin became irritated and I looked worse than before.

Even though I did not always agree with their tactics of trying to show me they all "cared," I still tried loving my family. Because they were still my family regardless of the good and the bad and as I was always told that no matter what, "blood was always thicker than water." In my case, a lot of times, I felt it was more water that was thicker than blood. I guess you are wondering where my biological father was throughout all this chaos. Well, we will get to that later.

From what I could remember, a year after we were living in South Carolina, my mother met her husband Greg. Then we moved to a little town called Maxton, North Carolina and after this move, it started a completely new set of problems. The one key thing I could remember about this man was that I hated him, and he was a very mean stepfather. What I mean by that is, he used to punch me in my back, just as my mother would do to me sometimes. Most of the time, it was for no reason he would ram his knuckles into my head, which eventually left me permanently deaf in my right ear later in my childhood, which is what they call nerve deafness.

In addition, Greg was also very scary because he had part of his thumb cut when he was little, and he always threatened or pinched me with that finger. Then, when I would purposely do something wrong, he would pull my ears or make me stand on one leg in the corner or I could never play with other kids in the family too long without having to come in the house and that made me label him as a mean stepfather.

I can remember a time when I was about 6 or 7-years-old, the house that we were living in, we had this old small brown suitcase and the thing with this suitcase was that I had to learn how to open it and that I had better do it right or else. But the problem with this suitcase was that it was really old, worn-out and rusty and every time I tried to open the locks, my fingers would hurt, but I had to open this suitcase no matter what, even if it took all night, and on this night, it took all night. Every time I tried and failed, Greg punched me, or I had to stand in the corner until I got it right.

In addition, what made me even more confused was how could my mother just sit there and allow him to do this to me and not say or do anything. The next day came, and of course, I had to try repeatedly until I got this suitcase opened. Well, the harder I tried, I did right before it became dark, and I finally got it open, I was so happy you would have thought I just got a brand-new toy. The thing was that I was so happy because I would not get punished anymore, at least for that, and finally got this stupid suitcase open.

I guess you were also thinking that I was the only child, well; it was only a few years after my mother married this man; I had a little sister who was the best thing that happened to my life and I thought about my mother's life. Why I said that was because when my sister Sheila was born, she was born with a birth defect, which was Cerebral Palsy. She was slightly mentally retarded and could not walk or move around very much; Sheila was wheelchair bound.

Most of the responsibilities of taking care of Sheila fell on me because I was the oldest sibling; we were 5 years apart in age. This would not bother me, but I was feeling like she was more my child than my sister, because I was always taking care of her for as long as I can remember, even when I got older. With Sheila's outstanding personality and amazing heart, you would have never thought that anything was wrong with her physically or mentally. Because once Sheila got old enough, sometimes we would be outside, and of course other kids would stare at her wondering what was wrong with her. Most of the times, I would have to say something in her defense, but then there were times Sheila would say, "why are you looking at me like that, there is nothing wrong with me, I'm just handicapped and can't walk, so stop looking at me like that."

There were moments Sheila would love to sing different songs to brighten up your day. Our favorite song was and still is, "you are my sunshine, my only sunshine." Sheila was the most joyous person to have around or a part of your life and she still is until this day.

Sometimes I think the Lord sent her as an angel for my protection. I used to think that my mother regretted having my sister and I because she always would treat us differently. She would always act frustrated and disappointed with us, because of Sheila's physical and mental condition, and my skin disorder that she constantly had to deal with.

Sometimes she would show it in her words or her actions. However, there would be times I would come to Leslie and say to her, "I love you," and she would often say that she did not love me. Leslie would often say to me she wondered why she was being punished with the children she had, and of course, me being a child, I often took that to heart and really felt that she did not love my sister or me. I thank God, because of my sister's mental state, He did not allow her to understand what was really going on in our family.

However, I remember that for a while, Greg had disappeared from our lives and that just left my mother with all the time to chastise me for everything and anything. I do not think that I can ever remember a time where my mother did not beat me for something, whether I did it or not.

There was this one time I can remember, we were in the house and I was being chastised for something that I did and instead of my mother just beating me as she normally did, she pushed me into the corner of a wall, which left a big gash over my eye. When this incident happened, I thought at first that maybe I deserved it, but what made it even sadder was when I went to the doctor and my mother told me I better not tell the doctor how this happened. I was told to tell him I could not see the wall and I needed glasses. However, deep down inside, I think that the doctor knew better. He kept giving me this look to say that it was okay to tell the truth. Because I was so afraid of what my mom would do to me, I stayed quiet. Unfortunately, I ended up wearing glasses until I was 12 years old.

THE MOVE THAT CHANGED IT ALL

About three years later, Greg appeared back in our lives. Once he returned, I thought maybe he changed for the better but only time would tell. There was one occasion, I was really tired of getting beatings for no reason, so I decided that if I would get chastised, let it be worth something. We were riding in the car; I was in the backseat and found some matches, so me being the child I was, I tried to light it and burn us up in the car. I remember my mom saying that she smelled smoke; she looked in the back of the car and looked at me, so I confessed to trying to light the match and burn us up. Unfortunately, it did not work, and I got a bad beating.

Then there was another time my mother was selling candy, so to gain friends at school, I used to steal her monies and candy and give it to the kids at school. My teacher finally found out what I was doing, and my mom found out so, this time, I got a terrible whipping from Aunt Tracey.

In my mind, I truly believed that if I constantly get beatings, I will make it worth her while and maybe make her feel a little better. Later, my mom, Greg, my sister, and I packed up and moved to Philadelphia, PA, the city of brotherly love, and I was praying and hoping that most of my problems with my mom and stepfather would end, but that was just too good to be true.

When my family and I first moved in Philly, I thought that this was a wonderful place to live and I was going to be so happy here, because when we moved to Philadelphia, we stayed with my stepfather's family. They lived in a nice quiet neighborhood. In addition, when we moved, it was around wintertime and there was a lot of snow on the ground, something I had never seen before or at least I did not remember seeing. Because in the South, wintertime did not produce any snow and when I lived in New York, I do not remember ever seeing snow.

Endurance is Victory

Well, I was wrong about my happiness doing a 360-degree turn and my mother and stepfather taking a new leaf. After about three months of being in Philly, I was having a lot of fun, of course, because we were living with my mother's husband's side of the family; people whom I had never seen before and didn't have any knowledge of how we lived our lives.

They were trying to put on a pleasant face and let this family see that we were a happy family when I knew otherwise. When we first moved in with the Browns, I felt like I was finally going to be a child again, and for a while that was true. The Brown's had a son, David, who was about a couple of years older than me.

David and I always hung out together, at least when he was going outside to play, because I was only about 10-years-old. I remember little about anything else about the stay there, except the fun times, and that did not last long in my life. After about six months, I was told that we had to move to our own house and I felt sad and hurt because I knew that our old lifestyle would begin again, as nothing would change.

Endurance is Victory

Once our six months was up, we moved to our own house and that i\was where the troubles continued to brew even more. We moved into a two-bedroom apartment on a street called Leidy Avenue, which was part of a terrible neighborhood, when I was about 11 or 12-years-old. Everyday kids constantly teased and taunted me about my skin, my personality, or my clothes in the neighborhood and school.

I felt that torture was worse here than it was in South Carolina because over there the people eventually got used to it, but when you move to the big city life, it is a whole different ball game, and everyone is not as understanding to the southerners. I was always running home crying to my mother about the kids teasing me and she would always send me back outside or ignore me. Leslie would often say she did not want to hear that noise, she would also say go out there and stand up for yourself, but it felt kind of hard when I did not have anyone in my corner or giving me moral support like I thought a mother supposed to do.

My sister Sheila and I did eventually make some friends with our neighbors next door who had a daughter by the name of Sylvia and her friends. Sylvia had two brothers, one of them was older than her and the other was younger. Every time I could go outside, I would always run over to Sylvia's house to play with her or Sylvia would come to our house.

Other times, Sylvia, Sheila, and I would just play outside because sometimes, being as though my sister was in a wheelchair, it would be very hard to get her up and down the stairs. But when we moved to Leidy Avenue, I tried to make a lot of friends regardless of my skin situation but sometimes that was not always possible, because I would always run into someone who would give me a little trouble because of my intelligence, my skin, or the way I dressed.

The whole time that we lived there, I only had one key person who I would constantly have problems with no matter what and her name was Girlie. This young lady was always in my face about something and we were constantly arguing. I would never fight Girlie because I was afraid to fight her or anyone else. I was not into fighting but I taught myself how to defend myself. When I first met Girlie, I thought we would become friends because we had one thing in common; she too had a brother who had special needs. I thought Girlie would understand some of what I was going through, but that did not happen. So, I would always call my cousin Iesha from South Carolina and tell her how this girl was treating me. I would always ask her to come up and get her for me when they would come and visit. After a couple of visits from my cousin Iesha, Girlie would eventually leave me alone.

Once we moved to Philadelphia; I had to take care of my sister even more than when we were in North Carolina. Every time I went outside, I had to take care of her. Mind you, she was in a wheelchair and that meant that there were a lot of things I could not do as a young child between the age of 10-12-years-old should be able to do. So, as a child, it limited fun activities with other children in my age group, but life still went on. Around the age of 12-years-old, I went to the doctor for a routine visit and that was when I found out that I was asthmatic and had completely lost my hearing in my right ear. After having so many breathing issues and constantly failing the hearing test that they gave me in school. Imagine you are sitting in the doctor's office and he is trying to figure out why you keep failing the hearing test. So, after further extensive tests, he found out that I had what they called nerve deafness, which was untreatable. The only help that I could get was to get an expensive hearing aid, which was like a microphone, but it would not restore my hearing, only amplify the surrounding sounds. Here is the funny part about this story.

When the doctor explained my diagnoses, he asked my mother if someone had hit me in the head and of course, her first response was "no." Then, I reminded her of how Greg used to push his knuckles into my head and the times she pushed me into the corner of a wall, so I felt like it kind of helped her memory, but with my mom, she ignored everything. Now along with having severe Eczema, I also had asthma, and nerve deafness in my right ear. I was also diagnosed with vertigo after a while.

THE FIGHT THAT I WOULD NEVER WIN

When I was about 12 years old, something terrible happened to me that changed my life forever. My stepfather raped me. Yes Greg, my mother's husband, and my sister's father, raped me! When this happened, I thought I was the worse child in the world to let my mother's husband do this to me. I thought I was never supposed to let something like that ever happen, because I was the oldest. Even though I was never taught what to do or how to respond, I just figured this should not happen to me. The way Greg approached was very different because I was in my bedroom and Greg called me in the living room to talk to me, of course, my mother wasn't home.

Still to this day, I think she was running around with the man that would later become her second husband, but we will talk about that later. I still cannot recall until this day where my sister Sheila was. I assumed she was in our room. Anyway, Greg told me that my mother was not satisfying him and that this would be our little secret. At that moment, I did not know what he was talking about until he made his move and I ended up on the floor, scared, not knowing what to do or what he would do if I tried to stop him. After it happened, I became scared and all I wanted to do was to tell my mommy, but it also scared me that if I told her, what she would do to me, or what he would do, or if she would even believe me. But I was a brave little soldier; I ran to her and told her everything that Greg did and said to me. At first, she did not believe me, but I guess she thought about it and she put him out.

Endurance is Victory

We went to court and after that, everything seemed to move so quickly. The only thing I can remember about my court ordeal was that I spoke with a lawyer and she told me all I needed to do was go to court and tell the truth and that he would not bother me anymore and it would be all over.

But before we even went to court, a lot of stress was placed on me, because along with me still going to school, I was constantly in and out of the lawyers and police offices or trying to go to counseling sessions to talk about what happened to me. When I first started going to counseling, I really felt that it was helping me get out my feelings about what happened and talk about my relationship with my mother, I was trying so hard to have with her.

It seemed like the more I wanted to go, the more my mother kept giving me negative feedback on me going to counseling by saying things like, "I don't know what you are going there to do, for it won't help" or "you talk too much, stop telling these people our business." After about a couple of sessions, my mother pulled me out because she thought I did not need the therapy anymore and she felt I should not be telling other people our business. In my mind, I thought it was not our business, it was my business, feelings, and thoughts of what happened to me and if I couldn't share them with my closest friends or family, then I could at least share them with a certified counselor or therapist. So, of course, I stopped, and I was not happy with it. I started thinking that maybe I was supposed to keep my feelings inside so no one gets hurt. But after the first set of sessions, I tried to go again and of course, I stopped, so I gave up and I never expressed my feelings to anyone, not even a counselor or psychologist ever again, because I was afraid of their response or what my mother would say.

Once the court hearing was over, a sigh of relief came over me because I really did not like Greg anymore. I thought he was a terrible man from the very beginning and now I was happy I would not have to see him anymore because of the bad things that he did to me. After the trial was over, I was told he was going to jail for about 5 to 15 years but could possibly get out sooner on exemplary behavior. During this whole time, I was feeling really lost and unwanted. The one true man I looked up to and loved with all my heart, which was my father, and whom I had never met but loved and wanted so much, was nowhere around, which was what I was told every time I even mentioned my daddy. Every time I asked my mother about my daddy, Richard, I was told by my mother that she did not know and that she did not care that he was a drug dealer and that he stayed in and out of jail and I was better off without him.

But I did not care because I knew he would protect me and he would never mess with me in a bad way; from what I was told by his family, I mean his mother, or his aunts and my family all told me he really loved and missed me. Especially because I was his firstborn child. But my mother still insisted there was no reason for me to see him. It did not matter to me who he was or what he did. He was still my daddy and I needed him because I knew my dad would get that man for doing what he did to me.

After I got through that ordeal, we continued to stay in the apartment. Then not too long after the trial, my mom met another man which, I think she was dating the whole time we were going back and forth to court and just using church as an excuse to leave the house and be with this man. But this man named Fred, my mother met, who eventually became her second husband and the father of her two boys, who supposed to be a former Police Officer, and a Preacher: A Bishop of a Church. Fred was not the man I thought he would be, and he was not a father figure in my eyes. This man also turned my mother into a Minister and she became a Reverend of his church organization.

At first, Fred seemed like an okay guy until time went on and I really got to know him, which did not take very long. By this time, I was about 13 years old and I felt my mom loved and cared about him even more than before, especially because he was not my sisters' father, he was not mine and he supposedly had money.

My mother was always with this guy. I started seeing the same pattern that happened with the first man, happening again with the second man, but me still being a child, I had to deal with it because I had no say in anything or did not have the right to say anything. The longer she stayed with this guy, the closer she became to him, to where she started sending me over to his house to cook and clean for him on weekends, while she took care of other things.

Endurance is Victory

You are probably wondering why a 13-year-old child was cooking and cleaning for her mother's boyfriend when she should do that herself? But again, me not knowing any better and thinking to myself that everything was fine; I really thought nothing of it.

After a few visits to his house, I thought maybe he was nice guy and that my mom finally found the right guy, right? Wrong! The next time I went to his house was the last time I ever wanted to go back because it happened to me again. Yes, this man raped me also, just like the first husband.

The way Fred approached me was by telling me he knew about what took place to me before with Greg and said, "that was wrong for what he did to you because he wasn't being a fatherly figure, but that this is how a father supposed to treat his daughter." Fred even said that my mom agreed this time and that it was okay for him to do this to me.

Mind you, I am was such an idiotic and a very naïve young lady and I really thought that maybe my mother really approved of this. This happened to me before and she really did not make a big deal out of it like I thought she would, so maybe I deserved it and she gave him the okay. So, after the first time, he finished his business, I ran home wondering what I was going to do this time. I thought, Should I tell my mom, was she going to believe me or not because it happened once maybe it cannot happen again?

And, if I told the cops again, they also probably would think I was lying and I was making all this up especially since Fred was a former cop, so I was told. I was feeling like there was something wrong with me, because this was not supposed to happen twice with two different men that my mom was with and supposedly loved them and they loved her, so I thought.

At that point I started thinking whether this time I led him on or maybe I wore the wrong type of clothes or said something wrong that made him want to do this to me. I also started thinking why all my mother's men were approaching me, what was wrong with her or what was wrong with me and why was she constantly choosing the wrong men. If only my dad was here, none of this would have happened and I would finally be safe.

Endurance is Victory

After about a month or two, this sexual thing kept happening every time I went to his house. I kept telling my mom that I did not want to go, but I could not tell her why, so she would still make me go.

So, one day, I was finally going to get up the nerves to tell her because, first I was tired of this happening and second, I was starting to feel very dirty and embarrassed because I was allowing this 300lb man to do this to me at only 108lbs and I felt as if I could do nothing to stop it.

When I finally decided that I was going to tell my mother, she told us we were moving in with him up to the Northeast section of the city. Once we moved in with Fred, I figured either he would stop having sex with me or we would have to move somewhere else, but I knew that was not going to happen.

After about a couple of months of us staying with him, I finally told my mother what Fred was doing to me and, also that he said that she agreed with it and that it was okay. At first, she had that look on her face like, "not again, I don't believe this, is she lying or what" but then she said that she was sorry and that she would talk to him and that she never told him it was okay.

Well, I guess eventually she talked to him but after their conversation, he came to me very upset. The next time Fred was alone with me, he started asking me why I said something to my mom about what happened and that she not supposed to know. So, I said to him, "well, you told me she said that it was okay, so I wanted to make sure." Then Fred said for me to never do that again because this was our secret and my mother did not need to be under any stress, especially since she was a schizophrenic; it would be my fault if she got sick again.

As time went on, he stopped physically messing with me. I guess that was because, from what I was told, he had a terrible heart and that he had a pacemaker, and it was hard for him to be very active after a while. But from the looks of it, the way he was always begging me to give him sex or do certain sexual acts, this would have been very hard to believe

After this, Fred would start messing with me mentally and emotionally and why I say this is because every time I would need something, whether it were clothes or money or whatever, I would always go to my mom for it and she would always say she doesn't have it.

It was always either he did not give her an allowance yet or she spend it on bills, and she would always tell me to go to him. This would be what I would always regret doing because when I would go to Fred to ask him for money, he would always say, "well, I can give it to you, but you know what I want from you and in order for you to get what you want from me you, know what you have to do for me."

Every time he would say that to me, I would find another way to get what I needed in order to avoid having any type of physical contact with him. But there were a few times I had to break down and let him do what he wanted with me. By this time, my mother was acting bizarre and this was her first stage or my first experience dealing with her schizophrenia and she was also pregnant with my first brother, but I did not know for a while.

What I mean by my mother was acting very bizarre; she was having me do strange things. Oddly, Fred seemed to always disappear when my mother would have her episodes. I can remember a time when my mother got so sick, she started throwing a lot of her good things away and then she would make me throw a lot of valuable items away.

What I mean by valuable, here is an example of my mothers' episodes. I had taken home economics in school and we had a sewing class where we had to make a skirt. This skirt was valuable to me, because it was one thing that I had accomplished that no one could take away from me. There was a time where we were in the house and she was still going through her motions and on this day was when she threw away my skirt. Leslie kept telling me that a lot of things were old, and I kept saying, "no mom, this is not." But she would scream at me and force me to say things she was throwing away were old.

On this day, I remembered my skirt being one of the items she was throwing away. I kept saying, "mom, it's the skirt I made in class, and it's new." Unfortunately, I can remember her screaming at me making me say that it was old, and she had to throw it away.

After that I cannot remember what else she said to me, but all I remember was that I made her so mad that she threw me on the floor, then slammed my head down so hard on the floor to where I thought that my head busted open. And can you believe that after she did this to me, she acted as if I was wrong for crying and screaming from being in so much pain? But my mother always said that this was our old life, and we were coming into our new life. At first, as a young child being afraid of her, I did not understand what that meant.

One day, my mom woke me up around 3:30 in the morning and told me to walk and stay up with her. We were walking down the street and as we were walking down the street, we walked right into a brand-new house that the construction workers were preparing for another family.

For some odd reason, the doors were open for anyone to walk inside. This was a house that did not belong to us and she said it was ours when I knew better, but because I was afraid of what she would do to me, I learned to just agree with her. That is another example. I can also remember a time when we were traveling on the city bus and she would bark at people and call them dogs, various types of dogs. Another day, we were on the back of the bus and she saw this White guy. She laughed and said to me, "Katrina, there goes a big dog, that's a Doberman pincher." Then she barked at him and instantly the guy heard her and became furious. Now, being a child, I was trying to protect both my mom and me, so I signalled to the guy on the sly that she was "crazy" so he would not mess with us. I pulled the cord quick for our next stop. These were the examples of living with a schizophrenic and no one knowing or even caring about what you are going through.

Now, I was 14 years old and I was old enough to work, so I found myself a job to take care of myself and provide for myself because if I did not, I was afraid that one day I would have to do what Fred wanted me to do.

Later on, I started hating myself for stooping down to that level and giving him what he wanted in order for me to get things I needed whether it were clothes or even money just to spend at the corner store. Even though Fred had stopped abusing me sexually, he started working on me mentally. Fred would always wait until my mom would leave and start playing with himself or masturbating in front of me. This would make me feel so uncomfortable to where, every time my mom would leave, either I would beg to go with her or find somewhere else to go, but every time I would leave, I would always worry about my sister Sheila. Since Sheila had cerebral palsy and could not walk or understand, in the back of my mind, I would pray that no one would bother her. I always tried to keep her safe and until this day, I still don't know if Fred or Greg, Sheila's father ever touched her; but only God and they know.

Well, this continued to happen for a while. Sometimes I would even run away to ask for help; always hoping and praying that someone would listen. I would either always get sent back home or my mom and Fred would find me. I can remember a time where I ran to my mother's aunt's house, which was my grandmothers' sister and even she turned me away after one night of staying with her.

The next morning, she told my mother where I was, but this was after I told her what was going on hoping that she would keep me safe. I found out quickly that she would not help me because my skin had a flare up and she didn't want me in her house or around the other kids with my skin problems, because she thought I was contagious, and she did not want me to deal with all of my issues I was experiencing at home. This was the way I saw it was because she really did not care, especially because I was a distant niece, and this was her first time seeing me since we moved here. I later discovered that she told other family members that she thought I was contagious, and she did not want me infecting the other kids, so she lied to get me out of the house.

This kept happening until one day, while in school, I met a guy by the name of Brian, who at the time I thought really liked me and would help me get away from this situation. Brian was 21 years old and at the time I was 14 years old, I know you think that he was kind of old for me to be dealing with a grown man, but he made me happy and he was also my ticket away from my mom, Fred and all this nonsense.

Brian really liked me regardless of my age or what my skin looked like, so I clung to him. For a while, he kept me occupied by either taking me out or I would just spend a lot of time with him, while I was in school or I would talk to him when I could on the phone. Oh yeah, when my mother met Fred, I had some freedom as far as the phone or going outside because the area that we lived in, there were not too many children in the neighborhood. I guess you can say that he had some kind of control over her. I even cut school to get away from home and spend more time with Brian. This lasted for as long as it could because Brian would help me do it and help me keep my sanity. But because I was only in the ninth grade and a straight "A" or "B" student, I did not want to mess that up.

You are probably wondering how I could spend so much time with him, but sometimes I would leave school early and I could do so because my grades were pretty good in school and I was never any problem, so the school never noticed that I left the building. I could spend as much time with Brian and I would tell my mom that I was going to the library when I was really going with Brian. Yes … I know, I was wrong for lying to my mom, but that was the only way I could do things and that I could stay away from home and stay away from Fred.

I finally told Brian about what was going on in my home and of course, he wanted to approach Fred, but I told him to let it go: I did not want him to worry about it. I told him I would not be there long. Once

Endurance is Victory

I met Brian, I figured Fred would back off, but he did not. I think he got a little jealous, because he use to listen to my phone conversations and tell me everything that he would hear, everything I would say to Brian and he wanted me to treat him like that, but of course, I would not.

As time went on, I found out that my mom was pregnant by Fred a second time and then, not too much later, I became pregnant by Brian at 14-years-old. Now I felt scared and relieved at the same time, afraid I would get in trouble once my mother found out, but I felt relieved because I could finally get away from Fred and he would not be able to taunt me anymore by saying crazy things or doing crazy things to me.

Eventually I told my mom and at first, she was hysterical, but then she asked me who the guy was, and I told her, and she asked me if he, the father, was going to help take care of the baby and me and I said "yes." Then Fred really did not believe me. So, he wanted to know for himself because he told me that this guy could go to jail for statutory rape, but I told him how was that the case if I consented to it. This was not like what happened before. After that, I looked at him and thought, "what do you think could happen to you if anyone ever found out the truth about you having sex with me anytime you wanted and you telling me this is how a father was supposed to treat his daughter?" Then Fred asked me for Brian's number to call him to ask him what he was going to do.

At first, I was kind of hesitant, especially because he was talking about getting Brian in trouble, but I gave him the number anyway. Fred called Brian and asked him what he was going to do about the situation and Brian said that he was going to take care of the baby and me.

Well, Fred was not too happy with the response. He tried to do everything he could to make Brian look like a bad person by telling him he was going to jail for statutory rape. When that did not push Brian away, Fred told me he checked Brian's record and found out that he had been in and out of jail. I guess he was trying to scare me, but I did not care. I still wanted to be with Brian because he really cared about me and that was my ticket away from Fred, my mother, and all this madness. The only one thing that my mom and Fred could do to keep Brian and I apart was to send me back to South Carolina to live with my aunt Tracy until after I had the baby, if not longer. The further I was away from Brian, the better Fred thought it would be. The last time that I saw Brian was when we talked about me going down South and he was very upset about me leaving, but there was nothing he could do, especially because he was also still living with his mother and of course I was still too young to live on my own.

THE DEVASTATION NEVER SEEMED TO END

Once I was in South Carolina, Brian and I kept in contact as much as possible, which made me feel so much better, but then we suddenly lost contact. Every time I would try to call him, I never got to speak with him because he was never home. I started writing him and he never wrote me back. I started feeling like I had lost Brian and that he did not want to be in a relationship because we lived too far from each other and he probably met someone else; remember he was older than me. The devastation affected me tremendously because I felt so loved by Brian and I really thought that we were going to build a future together, but now, he was gone forever.

While I was down South for that period, I never really went anywhere because every time I would ask, I was always told "no." They would say because I was pregnant, or my skin did not make me presentable enough. Sometimes I could go out with my cousin and at those times, I did have some fun. I could even go back to school, while I was there because I was getting really bored at home every day with nothing to do, so my Aunt Tracy put me in school.

Then the big day came, nine months later. I went into labor to have my baby and it was the most interesting experience I ever had. When I first realized that it was time, I started feeling this excruciating pain that I had never felt before. It felt as if someone had just punched me in my stomach very hard, repeatedly. The only person who was at home with me was my cousin Iesha. I told her how I was feeling but there was basically nothing she could do, so we called our grandmother who was not able to help us either. Looking back, I believe she just did not want to help. By the grace of God that day, I was going to the clinic anyway, so I just waited for the van to come and pick me up.

When we got to the hospital, they rushed me to the Labor and Delivery room and I was instantly hooked to all these different machines so they could monitor my baby. Once I got into the room and they hooked everything up, the doctor started saying something was wrong with the baby.

When I heard this, I was so scared that I was going to lose my baby and I kept asking the doctors if everything was going to be okay. But they kept saying, "yes, don't worry, just relax." As time went on, the doctors and nurses kept pulling out all of this medical equipment to monitor the baby more closely and kept whispering amongst themselves.

At that point I knew something was wrong and I heard the nurse say that she could not hear the baby's heartbeat. When they tried to do an ultrasound at first, they could not even find my baby. It was like the baby had disappeared for a couple of minutes then reappeared. I started crying because I was afraid that I would not have someone to love me for me and I love them. Losing a child scared me. I did not want to lose my baby even though I was too young to take care of a child because I was a child myself. But my baby would have been my comfort zone to help me deal with my crazy life.

The time came for me to deliver my baby and I started to think that everything was going to be okay and I was so excited because the doctors took care of whatever the problem was. But then, when I started pushing my baby out, I could still hear the doctors and nurses whispering amongst themselves and their faces not looking so happy.

Once I pushed out my baby, I did not hear the baby cry and I asked the doctors, "What's wrong, what did I have, why isn't my baby crying?" The nurse and doctors finally answered and said, "it's a boy." But the doctors still looked puzzled, and then they told me that I had a stillbirth. I asked what that meant, and they said my baby was born dead.

At first, I did not believe them, maybe more so because I did not understand how my baby could be dead if he was just moving inside me. I became so devastated to hear that the one thing that would have brought happiness into my life was taken away from me and I started asking myself what I did to deserve this: yes, another blow to my heart.

After I delivered my baby, all I could think of was that nothing was wrong with him, he was okay. Even though I knew my baby had passed away, I still held, cherished, and kissed him like he was still mine and still alive because when I looked at him, he just looked like he was sleeping peacefully. I had already picked out the name, Dominik, and had made plans for our life. Then I began thinking that I could never love him, or keep him for the rest of my life, or even his love for me with no doubts regardless of what I looked like.

I asked the doctor how all of this could happen. He said, if I would have gone to Labor and Delivered the day before, liked they instructed me to, they probably could have saved my baby. Unfortunately, my aunt Tracy would not allow me to go to my appointment, because she said she had other more important things to do and that nothing was wrong with me. When the doctor told me this, I partially blamed my aunt for losing my baby. The other sad part of this devastating news was that with all the family I had, no one had enough monies, so they said anyways, to give my baby a proper burial. So, the hospital staff placed my baby in the incinerator like a piece of trash. My aunt took pictures of my baby for my memories, but oddly those pictures disappeared. I truly believe my aunt kept them for herself.

Before I went back to Philly, I sometimes experienced depression, but no one really knew because I kept my feelings and emotions to myself. It seemed like my aunt Tracy thought I should be with someone no matter who it was, so she tried to hook me up with this man who was at least 35 years old, and mind you, I was only 14 at the time we met.

At first, I told her I did not want to talk to him because he was old and nasty, but as usual, she insisted I talked to him. This situation made me think that because you are living in the South, they have certain ways that they do things. This guy Larry not only was he older than me, but he was also dirty looking and always liked to ask me to braid his nasty hair. There were plenty of times, I remember my cousins teasing me every time Larry would visit, and I did not like this at all. I felt like the fool and the laughingstock of the family. I remembered when my little cousin Jared was like 2-years-old and we knew him for sniffing people's seats when they got up. He would smell Larry's seat and say, "Muffin, Larry stink, phooey," and everyone would always have a merry laugh at my expense about this old man.

By this time, I was definitely ready to go back home but I still was not able to get in contact with Brian to tell him what happened or even talk to him about how I was feeling inside. So, after I had the baby, I started making my own plans to go back to Philadelphia. But before I moved back to Philadelphia, my mother called down South, not to check up on me, but to tell my Aunt Tracy and I the most shocking thing ever that I was hoping and praying would never ever happen.

My mother and Fred went to New York and got married and the news crushed my entire world, a little more than the news about me losing the baby. I really could not believe that even after I told my mother that he raped me every time I went to visit him and even after moving in with him. After all that, I still could not believe that she would still marry this man. I felt like I would never get away from my situation with Fred or my mother, so when I got back to Philly. I had to get a plan together or I was going to be depressed, scared, and lonely until I could move out on my own and I was refusing to let that happen.

Once I got back and got settled, I found out that my mom was really getting sick with her schizophrenia and I could not understand why because she was having my second little brother. When she got married, I figured everything was going to be fine. But again, I was wrong; I found myself home more with my sister and my first brother.

Strangely, Fred was out more to avoid having to deal with my mom and leaving me in charge of everything. So, I was the one always home taking care of everyone: my sister, brother, and my mother. The sicker my mother got, the harder it was for me to deal with the whole situation. I could not control her or keep her away from me.

Even trying to run away would have been a solution but who would take care of my brother and sister. The reason I said that was because since my mom was diagnosed with schizophrenia paranoia and it became very hard for me to deal with the pressure of taking care of an adult, a handicapped child, a little boy, at 15-years-old. For example, there was this time, we were home alone, and my mom was at one of her worst stages, and again, I was by myself with her. We were in the house and she was just doing bizarre things and by that, I mean she asked me to do something and when I refused because I knew it was wrong, she would hit me.

During all this chaos, we moved again to a street named F in the boulevard. By now my mother had already delivered my other brother and was about to bring him home. Once my little brother came home, my mother had gotten so sick we had to put her in the hospital for schizophrenia along with post-partum depression from having the baby. I began feeling stuck here forever and with Fred, I could never leave.

My mother eventually came home after about a two week stay in the mental hospital and by this time, I felt I had a little more freedom but limited to do some things like going outside or to the movies or even sleeping over my friends' house and going to teenage parties. When we moved to our new home, I met some friends, but I still had problems with people teasing me about my skin and the clothes I wore.

Endurance is Victory

After this, I went back to school and met this great person who I thought was the best thing that ever happened to me, her name was Benita. I met Benita at school and later I found out that we both lived in the same neighborhood right down the street from each other. We became really close friends. Benita would always stick up for me at school or at home when other kids would tease me.

Finally, I had found somewhere I could run to as a safe haven because her mother treated me as if I was one of hers from day one. Also, being as though she was the most popular person in school, no one ever bothered me when we were together with her other friends and eventually, they did the same. Even when we would hang out at home, she was the same way. She never changed her personality or thought about me in a different way, even after I told her what I was going through at home.

I thought sometimes, God knew I needed a real genuine friend, sister, or a guardian angel and He sent Benita my way. Well, the longer we stayed in our new neighborhood, the more people I met. By this time, I had met another family and the son of this family, by the name of Derrick, became very protective over me in his own little way. Derrick was a genuine friend whom I thought at least for him being a guy and the lifestyle that he lived, I mean I was always spending time with him and his family.

Sometimes if you saw Derrick, you would see me or not too far behind but you and no one else would believe that we were only friends, because we had become sex partners. Sometimes Derrick would have other girlfriends or sexual friends, but when I was around, he never treated me like he did not wish to be bothered with me. So again, I clanged to another person besides Benita but in this aspect of my life, it was a protective male friend. And why I said that was because when I was in the 10th grade, I had a big fight with my mom and Fred and when I say big, I mean big.

One day, I was outside with my friends and it was an early day; it was not dark or anything, but what happened this day really opened my eyes concerning my mom and Fred, bigger than anything. Well, anyway on this day, I was outside hanging with my friends and my mother called me in the house. Once I got in the house, I automatically thought that I did something wrong which was usually the pattern when I was called in the house. Once I got in the house, I asked, "what did I do?" and my mother stated, "don't worry about it, just come in the house."

By this time, I was mad because I did not do anything. I was just outside, out of the way and I was being called in for basically no reason. Then my mom said, "you are coming in to eat," and I asked, "okay, after I eat, can I go back outside?" and my mother said "no." So I just snapped and started crying and I remember saying, "this is not fair," and my mom and Fred said I had to go to my room and not to come back out.

At that moment I became very rebellious and told them no and said that I was not going anywhere. So, my mother and Fred demanded that I go into my room and they followed me just to make sure that I went. My mother pushed me into the room and onto the bed and just jumped on me. Now mind you along with eczema and previously diagnosed with asthma at age 10, my mother held me down by putting her knees into my chest while Fred beat me with the buckle of his belt to teach me a lesson and to show me, he was in charge. Eventually, I fought my mom of off me, and I said to both, "I am leaving, and I am never coming back," and ran out of the house.

Of course, my mother ran outside and chased me down. She asked me, "what did you say," and I said, "I'm leaving and never coming back." The next thing I knew, my mom had punched me in the eye right in front of all of my friends and told me that if I wanted to leave, then I could go ahead. After this happened to me, I felt so embarrassed and humiliated. But remember earlier, when I said that I met another family and their son Derrick, whom, yes, I was having sex with, but he came to my rescue and he helped me get up. The first thing Derrick asked me was if I needed him to beat my stepfather up or was there anything he could do or if I needed him to get my mother, and I said, "no."

After that event happened, of course, I could not leave because I had nowhere to go. So, I just sucked it up and stayed in my room for the rest of the night. Well, the next morning I had to go to school and of course, everyone has seen it and my teacher sent me directly to the counselors' office. Once I got there, at first, I lied to my counselor so I would not get my mother in any trouble, but I eventually told my counselor and I begged them not to pursue anything because I had to still live there with my brothers and sister and if the system got involved, my siblings would get taken away and I did not want any of that to happen to them.

A BREAK THAT WOULD CHANGE MY PATH

Time had passed after that horrible incident and by then I had become even more promiscuous and was having more sex than I should have been, and of course, some of it was unprotected. By that time, I was in the 11th grade and discovered that I was pregnant again.

Even though I got pregnant, I still wanted to continue school. I always remembered my mom telling me she never graduated from High School because she was pregnant with me and she felt like I held her back. She always kept saying, "I was about to walk across the stage, but because I was pregnant with you, I couldn't graduate." So, I promised myself that I would not let that happen to me because my mom said she waited until it was almost time for her to graduate, then she quit school simply because she was pregnant with me, and I was to blame for her not graduating. So, I said to myself that if I ever got pregnant again, I would continue to go to school and try to achieve my dreams and goals.

Of course, I really wished that it was my decision, but again it was not. My mother told me I had to drop out of school and the excuse that she used was that I was a high-risk pregnancy because of my asthma, and I had to stay home until I had the baby. But all of that was not true at all. The main reason was so that I could babysit my brothers and sister while she took care of her business with the community center program that she and Fred were a part of, along with doing whatever else every day.

When I went to school to tell the teachers that I had to drop out, they were not too happy, so they called my mother, and we had a meeting to figure out another way for me to continue school. Of course, she stuck to her story for me to drop out saying it was because of my health, even though I knew different. Yes, I had terrible asthma but not to where I could not continue attending school. The counselor suggested

Endurance is Victory

I could go to a maternity school and of course my mother still said no and stated she did not have bus fare for me to get back and forth to school. When the school offered a solution for that and provided free tokens, her answer was still no.

Before I left school, I was an honor roll student, never got into trouble, and I loved school. It was the only time of the day that I was away from Fred and my mom because I still had problems with other High School kids picking on me. Once I dropped out of school, the first knock at my mother's door the next day was a truant officer sent to speak to my mom about putting me back in school because at 15 years old, I was supposed to be in school but as usual, she was not home.

When my mom came home, I told her that the truant officer came by and she still did not care and said, "I am still not going to send you back to school and no one can make me do it." I guess you are wondering about the father of my baby. Well because I was a little promiscuous and at first, I really did not know who my child's father was. I was with Derrick and another guy by the name of Kevin and I just figured that it was one of them. So, at first, I told Kevin and he was in shock, but he said nothing negative and did not push me away, but I did not want him to be the father and I knew he was not. Then I went to Derrick and at first, I thought he was okay with it, then suddenly he just did a straight 360-degree turn on me and told me I was lying. He said I was a "whore" and that he would never ever get me pregnant. Of course, I felt hurt and rejected because I would have never seen this coming. So, I told his family, hoping to get their support or hoping they would make him change his mind about me and the baby.

At first, it was very hard to do but I guess because I didn't have the baby yet, he tried to be cordial with me, at least, until I had the baby. Meanwhile, I was still being harassed by Fred even after he found out that I was pregnant again, but I guess because this time I did not have an involved baby father, he did not feel so threatened.

As soon as my mom would leave, Fred would still masturbate in front of me or ask me to have sex with him and I would always tell him no or find other ways to get out of it. He would even ask me to give him oral sex. Now imagine a 300 lb adult man and I was only about 115 or 120 lbs at 15-years-old, just lying there for me to give him oral sexual pleasure. When I would say "no" he would say "I know you can do it because I overheard your conversations with other guys over the phone about how you are going to make them feel good, so I know what you can do."

Fred also had the audacity to tell me he would play with me at night while everyone was asleep and the bad thing about that was that because I slept so hard and could only hear in one ear, I would never know if he was there or not. But I would remember there were some mornings I would wake up wet as if I went to the bathroom on myself, but I could never figure out why. He also told me things like he slept with his own niece and taught her how to please a man and even one of my friends or who I thought was my friend.

At that time, I felt so unloved by my mom, because I figured she knew everything that was going on and that she did not care. She loved this man so much that when she left me in the house with him, even after I would beg her not to, Leslie condoned everything that he did. She already knew about the incident at the other house and took no action. So, I became even more promiscuous even while I was pregnant because I was looking for love from anyone who could give it to me. I was looking for a way out of the situation, especially since I was not getting it from home or family members.

By this time, I was almost due to have my baby. When that special day came, my water bag broke and I told my mom thinking that she would know what to do. She just said that it was better for me to stay home because if I went to the hospital, they would send me back home, especially if I was not in any pain. And I thought that since she has had five children by now, she should know what she was talking about, so I went back outside to play like nothing was wrong. When I finally came back in, my water bag was still leaking, and I was told to just lie down with one of my sisters' wet pads and diaper, so I would not make a mess.

The next morning my water bag was still leaking, and when I called my mother, she finally said that I should call the hospital to see what to do and then she left, leaving me to figure it out. I called them and my nurse was so upset with me, she told me to come in as soon as possible but I told her I could not because I was home babysitting and that my mother was not home. The nurse said to me, "call your mother right now and tell her you have to come to the hospital because you could have a dry birth and that this is not a good thing for the baby." I called my mom and told her what the nurse said, and she said, "all right, go ahead." She told me she would be home shortly and that I could take the bus to the hospital.

Once she came home, which was around 3:00 PM, I left to take the bus to the hospital, and I guess you are wondering why my mother would not take her firstborn child and her first soon to be grandchild to the hospital? Well, I never asked, and I did not care. But before I went to the hospital, I put one of my sisters pampers on and left the house.

As I was walking to the bus stop, my very best friend Benita, who had been there with me through all my trials, asked me where I was going. I told her that I was going to the hospital to have the baby. And at first, she said, "where is your mother?" And then I heard her say, "never mind." Then she said as soon as her mother got home that she would meet me there because she already knew the situation with my mom and Fred.

Endurance is Victory

When I got to the hospital, I went right upstairs to see the nurse and at first, she fussed at me and then she put me in a room right away. As I was waiting for the doctors to come, the nurse asked me who was here with me and I told her no one, but my girlfriend was on her way to just let her in when she arrived. The doctors came in and checked me and said that they were almost ready. When I heard that, I felt so relieved because I did not want a repeat of the first baby, but I was also still fearful of what could happen. Benita finally arrived and I was so glad to see her. I told her everything that was going on and we just waited as we laughed and talked about a lot of different things.

Then, after about an hour had passed, the nurse came in to check on me and she kept asking me if I felt the contractions coming and I kept telling her "no." So, she said she was going to give me something to push it along and would be back in about twenty minutes. Twenty minutes passed and I started feeling the contractions a lot more. When it was time to have my baby, a couple of minutes went by and Benita and I witnessed a beautiful little girl being born and what made me even happier was when I heard her cry, and I did not hear or see the doctors mumbling or looking puzzled. I then knew, everything was fine.

Endurance is Victory

When I first came home with Angel, I was so excited. I imme- diately found Derrick who was with his brother. I showed him our beautiful baby girl and his brother Richard instantly said, "man, that's your baby, she looks just like you bro." Derrick laughed and said, "man, that's not my baby." His brother said, "man, don't be like that, you know that's your baby."

Again, Derrick was still denying our beautiful little girl and it hurt me so much to my core. How could he deny such a beautiful baby? He knew we were always together and had a lot of sex even when I would try to be with other guys, I always came back to Derrick because I was in love with him and he did not know it or probably cared. I guess because we were young, and he was not thinking about love.

Then, one day, I was going to the corner store with my baby and the Korean guy in the store said, "Oh, you had your baby, she's so pretty, where is her father." I said, "I didn't know." The next moment Derrick walked in the store and the Korean guy said, "there he is, you have a beautiful baby." Derrick came in, started laughing, looked at my baby and said, "that ugly baby is not mine" and walked out of the store.

Endurance is Victory

At that moment, I felt so humiliated, so small, and unworthy. All I wanted was for me and my baby to be loved and appreciated by the one person who I thought loved me or at least cared about me. After Derrick embarrassed me so badly, the Korean guy said that he was sorry and that I would be fine, and I just left the store.

After that humiliating incident, and for my Angel, I started adjusting my life, by first going back to school to get my High School Diploma and to get another job so that I could take care of my child and second by trying to clear up my skin. This was not a simple job, not because I could not do it, but because my mother stood in my way with every chance she could afford.

What I mean by that is, every time I needed her to watch Angel for me, she would either say no or if she would babysit her, she would wait till the last minute then change her mind or refuse for me to let anyone else watch her, especially if she did not know them. I can remember times when I was about to leave to go to school or work and she would tell me she could not watch Angel, so I would have to run around and find someone else to watch her. Then, if I did that, she would argue with me about who was watching her because she did not know them, or she did not trust them. I would constantly go through this until I got tired of it. The next time I went to school, I started talking to the counselor about my situation and I asked her if she could help me find somewhere to stay and she said that she would help.

Time went by and I had lost contact with Benita because she had graduated and was going to college. I did not have anyone that I could confide in or look out for me. After about five months, I had already turned 16 years old, and the counselor at the school told me that there was this shelter called "Project Heaven" for single women and children.

She signed me up, considering my home environment. But this place was not just any kind of shelter, it was almost like I had my own little apartment and we just shared the kitchen area. Of course, they had rules just like anywhere you move to in life, because the Catholic Association ran them, and they had an image to keep up with. I ran home to tell my mother the splendid news and of course she acted like she really did not want me to leave, but I knew she was happy because she did not fight hard to keep me there.

PREPARATION TO HAVE SOME PEACE

As I was waiting to hear from Project Heaven, life at my mom's home just became unbearable. While I was trying to figure another exit plan, I found out that I was pregnant again. This time I found out I was having a son. By this time, my aunt Tracy and her children had moved to Philly, so I asked her if I could stay with her until I could move into Project Heaven. During my stay with Aunt Tracey, I had some peace and happiness; it felt sort of like when I was younger, and we all played together.

While I was staying with Aunt Tracy, I was finally being treated like a human being. I started working on how to clear my skin up, not just for myself, but also for my daughter and now, my second unborn child I was carrying. At first, it was really hard to keep my skin clear because there would be times where someone or something would worry me and my skin would flare up again, but with persistence and with the help of my aunt and cousins, I never gave up.

Endurance is Victory

There were times I was feeling like I should be on my own because my Aunt Tracy took more than I could give. By this time, I was in college, working, and trying to build my income for my move to Project Heaven. As a golden rule, I learned you cannot live anywhere for free when you are staying in their home. So, I would give my Aunt Tracy whatever I could afford to pay my way while I was living in her home.

However, with Aunt Tracy, she loved gifts or extra money just because that was who she was. So, because I am a giver, anything she would ask for, if I could, I would buy her. Hats for the church, pretty dresses, whatever she wanted, I would try to provide for her. I remember my cousin Iesha and her brothers would always say, "Mommy like you more than us," and I would feel bad and thought, I should not be doing this. I would always have to defend myself with my cousins and convince them that I was not trying to take their place.

Over time, I was feeling like I was being used by Aunt Tracy, so I had to figure out a way to cut back on the giving and causing no issues. Somehow, over time, I would always give Aunt Tracy a reason

Endurance is Victory

I could not buy a hat or that special gift she wanted. I would tell her I had to move soon, and I could not save my monies if I kept spending extra money.

She did not like that but she accepted it. While I was staying with Aunt Tracy, the time was coming for me to deliver my son. Before this time, when I went to the doctor, I remembered getting three different delivery dates, first it was December 7th, then the 12th, then the 17th, and then a nurse said the 24th. I remember looking at the nurse thinking, "I'm not having my child around Christmas time, that is not happening."

The due date was here. I can remember as clear as day. We were out Christmas shopping on 5th street near the Olney/Fern Rock area on Christmas Eve and I kept saying I was hungry. We stopped by this restaurant that sold rotisserie chicken. I was feeling contractions but because I wanted to continue to shop, I kept on about the night and waited until I got back home.

Later that evening we were home sitting around the house laughing and enjoying the evening. Then out of nowhere, I said, "Aunt

Tracy, I'm having contractions." Aunt Tracy looked at me and laughed, then she asked, "Muffin are you sure, because I'm not going to the hospital?" For a split-second, thoughts of when I lost my baby at 14-years-old came rushing across my mind. I said, "Aunt Tracy, I'm serious, I am having contractions, I'm ready to go to the hospital."

Aunt Tracy said, "do you have your trans pass because if it's a false alarm you can take the bus back home." I told her I had my trans pass but I was having contractions and it was for real. We got in the car and were off to the hospital. Once we arrived at the hospital, they checked me in and the doctor examined me and said, "well, I guess we're having a Christmas baby." I looked at him and said, "no, I'm having my baby after Christmas because my aunt is cooking." The doctor laughed and said, "okay."

Aunt Tracy looked at me and said, "I have to go home, are you going to be okay? I said, "yes" and she left. God blessed me with a beautiful and healthy little boy that I brought into this world. He was born on the best day of the year, Jesus Christ, the son of God's Day on December 25th, at 8:36 am. After this miracle, I started thinking maybe there will finally be a glimmer of hope for me. From that moment on, I thought God had His eyes on me and things were finally looking up for me.

But the only sad thing was that his father knew nothing about this special miracle, because I was afraid, he would treat me like my first child father did, so I delayed telling him. And of course, again I was left alone to take care of two children on my own, with no help from their fathers.

My mother Leslie was not there either and again another child I brought into this world and my mother was not here to support me. While I was in the hospital with Malachi, my Aunt Tracy called me to tell me that my daughter Angel was very sick, and she did not know what to do. So, I told her to take her to the hospital and we found out that she had contracted pneumonia and was admitted to the hospital. During this time, I was worried about my daughter and frustrated I - could not be with her because I had just had her brother and because I was a high risk of asthma, I could not go visit her.

Unfortunately, while in the hospital, recovering and waiting to take Malachi home, he was also admitted because he contracted meningitis while in the hospital and taken away from me. This was a stressful time that I had to deal with alone. Aunt Tracy had her family and my mother just did not seem to be available. Eventually, I was well enough to go visit Angel while Malachi was healing and recovering from meningitis.

Finally, before they discharged me, Angel was well enough to come home. Then, I started focusing on healing quickly and making sure that Malachi was well enough to come home as well. After this ordeal, all I wanted to do was go back to Aunt Tracy's house, hold my babies, and focus on moving into my own apartment at Project Heaven.

THE MOVE AND MORE DEVASTATION

So, it was final. A month later, I moved out of Aunt Tracy's house; I was so happy I did not know what to do. Once I moved into Project Heaven, I learned very early that there was a lot of responsibility in being on my own, but I didn't care because if I wasn't with my mother or Fred, I was amazing.

Endurance is Victory

Project Heaven, which was a shelter for women and children who came from unpleasant situations, would help you get your life together, so where I lived was great. Living at Project Heaven, I had a lot more freedom compared to being at home and they really helped me out tremendously.

This program had a childcare center on-site, so I did not have to go anywhere and find someone to watch my children. The most important thing was that I did not have to deal with my mother and Fred and that made me feel even more at ease and safe. I had lived in Project Heaven for about eight months and I had never felt so much at home. I know this is a bad thing to say, but looking at my situation, when I was at home, I felt no real genuine love and was never wanted. But at Project Heaven, it felt like I belonged, even with my children and all my issues.

The glorious thing about this place also was that they helped me to be an independent woman with children at such a young age. The staff helped me to find a new apartment for my children and myself. Unfortunately, because I had broken one rule, I was told I had to leave earlier than planned and I refused to go back to my mom's house. I asked Aunt Tracy if I could move back in with her until my approval for public housing was ready and she said that was fine. I was still communicating with my mom and she knew where I was and she did not care, as long as I was happy because she and I knew I would never come back there, hopefully, with the Lord's help soon, especially as long as Fred was there.

After about three months later, I received a letter of acceptance, a letter for me to move into my new home. It was time to go through the application process and selecting a place to live. The only bad thing that I can say about this place that I was moving into was that it was a Public Housing Development (The Projects).

At first, when I was told that was where I was moving to, I cried like a baby because I was afraid to live there since I heard so many bad things about the projects and the neighborhood. Also, because from all those years of living in Philadelphia, I knew what type of life most of the people who already lived there lived. I heard a lot of horror stories and I did not want to subject my children to that environment, because

Endurance is Victory

I wanted better for them and myself. But, talking to other people about my new place of residence, gave me a little more insight of what to do and what not to do and how I could live there and not be a part of that lifestyle. A woman once told me, "It is not where you live but what you make out of it and also you have to crawl before you can walk."

There was a time while I was staying with my aunt when my mother asked me to come over. She had something very important that she had to discuss with me. Once I got over there, I thought that something happened, well, it did not, but I received another shocking bit of news. My mother and Fred dared to ask me if Fred could put his name on my daughter's birth certificate and be my child's father since she did not have one in her life and the one that I thought was the father really would not take care of her.

In addition, my mother said, "that way, Fred would provide for your daughter no matter what." Now, mind you, first, my mother agreed to this craziness; second, they were her grandparents; third, how would it look for my child's step-grandfather to be the father unless he admitted he molested me, and my mother also knew it and consented to it.

He was not the father of my child; I stopped him from raping me long before I became pregnant, there was no need for concern if he was the father at all. Well, of course, I told both no way, I was not that crazy and desperate. At first, I kept questioning them, mainly my mom how and why she could agree to this request. Also, how would it look to my little brothers that their father's name was listed as the father on their niece's birth certificate?

After this conversation, I refused to go back to stay with them. I can remember a time when my baby brother was around 4 years old and my mom decided finally to get him circumcised, which was odd to me. However, after the procedure, she asked me to make sure I watched him, changed his bandages, and put medicine on the area like he was my child. I promise you I was uncomfortable with this, but because my mother forced me, I had no choice.

Endurance is Victory

After the fiasco of her asking to put her husband's name on my daughter's birth certificate, I felt I needed to stand up for myself and my children since no one had our backs.

Well, before I moved into my apartment, my mother had a big tragedy that happened to her and I was told that I needed to put aside my differences and feelings and be her support system. I was at school one day and I received a call from my aunt asking me to come home and that it was an emergency.

Initially, I thought that something had happened to my daughter, son, or one of the other children in the house but once I got home, I was just told the most shocking thing ever. I was told that my mother's husband, Fred was in the hospital. He had a heart attack and it looked like he was not going to make it. When I was told this news, my first reaction was a sigh of relief (not meaning to be inconsiderate of the situation), but I was thinking more like, I will never have to get harassed again even when I visited him. But being the type of person I am, that attitude did not last long. When my aunt said this to me, my response was, "so what do you want me to do, I'm not going to the hospital. Do you remember what he did to me?" And my aunt's response was, "I know how you feel but you must be there for your mom, your brothers, and your sister because they need you right now and you have to put those feelings aside."

Well, I did the right thing. I went and visited him and felt terrified and sad at the same time. While I was watching him in the hospital, I had a weird feeling come over me and I became so frightened when I got to his room. At first, I did not want to go in because I would get squeamish when I see a lot of tubes in someone and I did not want to face the inevitable, but I did, which was watching this man die right in front of my eyes. I felt a sigh of relieve, I finally did not have to deal with him anymore.

As I watched Fred lie in that hospital bed, I had a lot of thoughts going on in my mind. Like first, why I am crying over this man who had made my life a living hell, then about how would I feel if that were me in that bed? I also thought the Lord did not teach me to wish anything bad, on any man or woman. But I was thinking about how he treated me. Eventually, a couple of days later, Fred died and while I was there supporting my mom during her time of grief, I kept asking myself, "where was the support from you when I needed it after I told you what he did to me and what Greg did."

But I had to let bygones be bygones because this was my brother's father and I didn't want them to know or see what was going on. While we were preparing the funeral arrangements, I was really praying that my mom and I could finally be close, like a mother and daughter are supposed to be. It lasted for a little while because after Fred's funeral my mother found out about a lot of his little dirty secrets, from him still being married to other women, having kids the same age as my brothers, to even as low as her so-called friend (supposedly a friend of the family) having relations with him behind her back for money and that same person was the person with him the day he had the heart attack.

My mother was really going through a rough time emotionally after finding out what type of man she had really married and during this time, we had finally had about an hour of a mother to daughter talk for the very first time in my life without us being at each other's throat until things got too deep for her. I could finally tell her how I truly felt about Fred and for her not to worry about being punished for what I said and that everything would be okay. I even told her how he told me about him having sex with one of my friends and how he told me he even showed his own niece how to have sex.

At first, I thought that my mom really did not want to believe that she had married a man like this, and I really thought she may have had some doubts, but she would never admit that to me. Until this day, I still believe that this was what pushed my mom over the edge about Fred.

This was enough proof that the man she loved and basically idolized so dearly, more than her own children (or at least her daughter), was no good from the very beginning. Once this ordeal was over, I still stayed with my aunt and continued to go to school and work.

After the death of Fred, my mom was really taking it hard, to the point where she got sick again and me being me, I tried to avoid it as much as I could. So, I moved back in with my mom briefly until I got my apartment, just to help her out, and again, that was the wrong decision. As time went on, my mom was herself again, meaning being strict, and I still could not go anywhere. I could not even get a key to the house when I would leave to go to school or wherever.

So, I felt like a kid all over again at 16-years-old with two children. I kept calling Project Heaven and the Housing Authority to find out the status of my apartment so I could hurry and move out before I snapped at my mom. So, I decided to move back in with Aunt Tracy because I really could not take the pressure of living with my mom. About three months later, I finally received a call from the Housing Authority that my apartment was ready and that I could move in. I finally made my transition into my new home with my children, which was something that I thought would never ever happen, but it finally did.

Once I moved into my apartment, I knew I was free from my mom, Fred, Greg, and anyone else who treated me wrong. By then I had turned 17 and I could finally say that I was an independent woman and I said this because now I was providing for my children and paying my own way through life, while still attending college and working. During my stay at this housing development, I tried to stay to myself as much as possible so I would not cause any problems with any other people in the building. I had some rocky times while I was there, but I attempted to work out my problems so I would not have to go back home to live with my mother. Living on my own had its difficulties, but I learned a lot about life's lessons that there would sometimes be some turmoil but nowhere near as bad as living with my mother.

I was constantly in and out of different relationships trying to look for the "right" man that would want me and my children but that also meant that I would not date anyone who would not accept my children because we came as a package deal. I can remember there were times I would meet guys and I would tell them I have two children and I would either get a remark like, "what time do they go to bed" or "I can't mess with you if you have children."

So, I only chose men who liked children and if I introduced them to my children, my kids would have to like them also, especially because I did not have that as an option. But keep in mind, even though

Endurance is Victory

I was still promiscuous, I was still very selective on who was around my children and who was not.

When I was about 18 years old, my mother had gotten sick again because of the stress of losing her husband along with other things over some time where it took a big toll on her. I had to take on the responsibility of making sure she did not harm herself nor my brothers and sister.

I decided that in order for her to get the help that she needed, I had to put her in the hospital and that was what I did, eventually. At first, I felt so bad that I would have to put her in the hospital, but I felt that was the only way she was going to get help. She had gotten so sick and depressed to where she would not take her medicine or even communicate with anyone, even me.

Normally, my mom would think that everyone was her enemy and everyone was against her, but she would never treat me like that. Then there was one time where my mom wandered off and no one knew where to find her, and she left my sister and little brothers in the house by themselves. No one even knew about them until a neighbor finally realized that the boys were not going to school after about a week, then she notified my Aunt Tracy and me.

During this time, I felt I could not control the situation anymore, so I did what they call an involuntary admission (also known as a 302), which is when you involve the police, and they make them go to the hospital because they consider them to be a danger to themselves and others. I know you are wondering why I had to go to those extremes, but my mom was at one of her worst stages I had ever seen. Once she was in the hospital, I knew they would take care of her.

One day, while visiting my mother at the hospital, I met a guy that worked there as a security guard. I still had very low self–esteem about myself. My skin flared up again due to me being stressed about my mother and other problems I was having. I also started feeling like I would never find the right guy who would accept me regardless of what my skin looked like, even though I was working very hard to keep it looking clear sometimes and believe me it was very hard. Well, this guy, John introduced himself and I thought that he really did like me, until later in the relationship, when I felt very different about him. When I first met John, there was no attraction, but since he seemed to like me regardless of my situation with my mom and me having two children, he still seemed to not care about all of that. My Aunt Tracy basically pushed the issue that he liked me especially because of how I looked. She said no one was going to accept me right now with my skin being bad, so I made myself like him. During our relationship, John spent the night at my house a lot until, eventually, he just ended up moving in; an arrangement I did not plan.

Suddenly, he kept bringing his things every night he came, along with his video games and the next thing I knew, he was living with me. My daughter was two years old and my son was a year old. Again, my children's opinion of a guy even at that age really mattered to me. I noticed how John became a real child-like individual to the point where my daughter would really get aggravated and would not play with him because he played just too much to be a grown man. Now, in the back of my mind, I started thinking that he would do something crazy to my kids especially, my daughter. After that, I would tell him to just stay away from the kids because they did not want to be around him, and I did not feel comfortable. I know you are probably thinking why I was still with this guy, but it seemed like I just could not get rid of him. The only reason I was still with him was because while I was dating John, I had to have surgery on my knee, and I needed help around the house because I had to be off my feet.

While I was on bed rest, I was still looking for different employment and me being me, I got a call for a job interview. I explained the situation of me being on crutches to the receptionist and she stated it was fine, I could still come if I was able. So, I asked John if he could watch the children while I went to the interview and he said yes. This day was one of the worst days of my life because when I asked John to babysit for me: I never would have thought that it would lead to a tragic and stressful day. I went to the interview and after it was over, I called home and I got no answer. So now I am wondering what was going on and why no one was answering the phone.

Later, as I was traveling back home, I received a page from the housing manager. I called her back and she told me that my children were in the house by themself. So, by now, I am freaking out. First, I was scared that I was going to get in trouble for leaving my children at home by themselves and something could happen to them and second, I was wondering where John went because he told me he did not have to work that day. And he promised he would watch my children for me.

This was the first time I had ever asked him to watch my children and I regret asking him to do until this day. While I was on the phone with the housing manager, I tried explaining to her why I was not home and thank God that I could calm the situation and the manager understood and did not call social services on me.

But I still worried about my children and knowing that it was going to take me an hour to get home, I tried to call everyone that I could think of to check on my children. I could not get in contact with anyone even my mother, and till this day, I still do not remember what excuse she gave me, but she did not help.

So, I just prayed that the Lord would keep my children protected until I returned home. Eventually, I got home to my children and they were still there and alone, safe and sound with no harm done to them. I made some phone calls to locate John and to find out where he was, and I found out that he was at work. I called him at work and gave him a piece of my mind. I told him he did not care about me nor my children because if he did, he would not have left them in the house alone. Especially since he had so many other options if he had to go to work, such as day care or even his own mother but he chose not to use those choices. So, I told him to come and get his things and that I never wanted to see him again or for him to ever come around my children for as long as he knew me.

ANOTHER LOVE IN ANOTHER PART OF MY LIFE

After that ordeal, I forgot about needing help around the house while I was on crutches, so I focused on getting myself better. I focused on taking care of my children and getting back to work. About several months had passed and I met another guy, Reggie, who I really thought was the one, and by this time, I was about 20 years old and he was about 27 years old.

I was introduced to Reggie through my cousin Iesha because she worked with him and Iesha knew what I was going through with my skin condition and everything else in my life, so she thought he would be the right person for me. The primary reason was, believe it or not, Reggie had eczema just like me, but he was worse off than me, so instantly, I became attracted to him. When I met Reggie, I gave him a brief synopsis of my life and gave him a choice if he still wanted to be with me, and believe it or not, Reggie did not hesitate to say "yes."

During our relationship, we became very close. He even referred me to the dermatologists he was seeing, and I went. But what really made me fall so in love with Reggie was when he met me, he was having problems with his girlfriend, but still kept spending time with me. He also worked in a facility with adults that was just like my sister and he was very proud of his job. He especially got along very well with my sister Sheila, which really stole my heart and Sheila's response to him mattered even more. Reggie opened my eyes to so many things that I missed out on even at 20. He brought me around a lot of his family where they accepted me, and the most important thing was that my children adored him.

While I was dating Reggie, I was still in college about to grad-uate, and I can remember this was the second-best thing that happened to me. Again, my mother was nowhere in sight. I was in college to achieve my associate degree in Business Programming with a minor in Data Processing. By this time, I started having more confidence in myself because even though I was not in the situation I was in, I could still achieve the goals that I had set for my life. I was not about to make the same mistakes my mother claimed that she made with my sister and myself.

Again, for the fourth time in my life where a significant event happened in my life, it was someone else there to take her place again. Sitting right there in the stands was Reggie and his Aunt Judy, who took the time out of their busy life to attend my graduation from college and that made me the happiest person in the whole wide world. Of course, with me, happiness never lasted too long, because after about four months after graduation, I had again received another blow to the heart. Reggie had given me some very disturbing news. The news he gave me was that he was moving to Florida, which was not so bad until he told me he was going with his ex-girlfriend, the same one who was treating him like crap, and he was trying to get away from. Later I found out that he actually left with her. I felt so devastated that I did not know what to do. I felt betrayed again. I also felt that I did everything I could to keep this man happy and this was the thanks I got.

Well, once Reggie left, I felt that my life was over, and I had nothing to live for. The reason I say this is because I thought I had finally met someone that truly loved me for me, and my children and we had this one major thing in common: our skin. When I met Reggie, I really thought that we were soul mates. Even though we did not have the same family problems, we had the same skin problems and Reggie was my true inspiration in dealing with people and their rudeness to something they did not understand. When we were together, we meshed so well together as a couple, at least so I thought.

Once time passed, I had finally gotten over Reggie in my own way by sending a "goodbye forever" letter and telling him how I truly felt about him leaving with this woman. After that, I resorted back to dating different men again. I also used to call what we called the "Party Line" where you could meet different people and maybe hook up with them. Eventually, I met a couple of guys who became just my friends;

nothing intimate. After Reggie and the Party Line, I never met the "right guy" for me.

After Reggie had moved, and I was finally getting over the heartbreak, one day my phone rang, and I had the greatest phone call of my life. My father David had called me for the very first time in my life, after 21 years. Yes, it was the happiest day of my life; I was talking to my dad. We talked for hours trying to catch up on his life and him catching up on mine.

We also talked about what happened to me with Greg and Fred. He told me about my other brothers and sisters, although I had already told him I had met two of my sisters and one brother, but my father had 7 children, including me: five girls and two boys. The only thing was that I had to wait before I could see him because he was in jail and he was waiting for a weekend pass to come and see me.

After my dad and I finished talking and catching up, I called my mother to tell her the good news but to her it was not good news. The first thing that she said was, "I hope you are happy that you finally talked to that man you would not give up on." My response was, "I thought you would be happy that I finally found him." Well, I told her that in a couple of months he was coming to visit. We talked every other week until he came to see me and the time came quickly. I went to the train station to meet my father for the very first time in 21 years of existence on this earth. It was an awkward meeting at first, because I constantly asked what my dad looked like and everyone often said he looked like me.

However, when I went to 30th Street Station to pick him up, I saw this big guy who looked nothing like me, or so I thought. The reason I said this was to me, I was not very beautiful, and he was heavy, and I was skinny, and my mom always said that my dad was very slim. This was one of the happiest days of my life.

Once I picked up my dad and we went to my house, he saw my children and then I took him to my mother's house. When we got there, at first my mother acted like she did not want to see him, but I could see it in her eyes, she still loved my father after all those years. Once my dad went back to jail, we still tried to keep in contact, but it was kind of hard, especially with me never being home and not able to call him whenever I wanted to.

A couple of months had passed and the housing development that I was living in was about to go under renovation and I had to move to another development across town. But before I left, I had another shock of my life. I finally ran into Brian, the father of my very first child I lost.

At first, I was so ecstatic to see him again; then all the old feelings started coming back again. I told him about the baby boy that we lost and of course, he became very upset to hear that. He said that if he would have stayed here this would have never happened and said, "maybe I wouldn't have been with the family that I made."

But I told him that things happen for a reason and maybe it was for the best. At first, we tried to start something up, but because he was a married man, I knew it would not go anywhere but it was worth a try. Eventually, we just remained friends and held onto our memories. Again, I had to make a huge decision in my life.

Endurance is Victory

My mother was getting sick again and I just could not deal with the pressures of taking care of my children, working full time, going to school full-time, taking care of my brothers and sister and still having a life. Yes, my Aunt Tracy was there, but help-wise, she could only do so much.

Then there were sometimes I felt she did not really want to help, especially because this was my family and my problem. I mean, we would take turns taking care of my sister, but it became a big strain on both of us. So, I called my mother's mother Julia and explained the situation to her, and she suggested I bring her back down South to stay with her and she would take care of her and the kids. I figured that would be a great idea, not only would she be with her mother, but all her sisters and brothers too, so I took her down there. After I came back from South Carolina, I prepared myself to move into another house.

Once I moved to the other side of town, I met a guy that I sort of liked and I thought he liked me, but the only difference with him was that he was of the Muslim faith which meant that eventually, I would not be the only one, because when you get involved with a person of the Muslim faith, especially, a man, you are not the only woman in his life. Isaac and I were together for a good while and I thought it might be the beginning of an alright relationship. Well, while we were dating, I was still very cautious in getting too serious with him. I did not want to end up getting hurt again, so yes, I was still seeing other people just in case it did not work. But Isaac never even knew the difference, or he just did not care.

One night, I became bored and Isaac was not coming to see me, I did not feel like any other company coming over, so I visited a male friend of mine thinking it would have been fine. Well, that again was the biggest mistake of my life. It happened to me again. I went over to Joseph's house to sit and watch a movie with him and again for the third time; another man violated me.

All I remember was that one minute, I was sitting on the chair and then the next, I was on the floor begging for my life. I remember it like it was yesterday. Joseph asked me if we could have sex. At first, I thought he was joking, and I remember saying to him, "stop playing, you know we are just friends and I don't even see you like that." But Joseph just laughed and said, "I am serious you know I want more."

At that moment, I thought to myself, "I will not let this happen to me again. I am a grown woman now and I can defend myself." But before I knew it, Joseph grabbed me. I tried to fight him off me, but he was bigger and stronger than me. I found myself on this man's floor, wrestling and trying to fight him off me. I remember him telling me to stop fighting and to let him do what he wanted to do to me. So, I told him, "no, I am going to scream if you don't get off of me." But Joseph did the most frightening thing ever, which was pulling out a knife and putting it to my neck as he said, "just lay there and enjoy it and let me do what I want, or I will cut you." Unfortunately, I was indeed afraid for my life, not knowing if he was really going to kill me.

After Joseph finished his business, I jumped up and put my clothes on, but before I left, I said to Joseph, "I hate you, I hope you catch AIDS and die, and I never want to see you again." I drove home so fast; I could not see straight. I almost crashed my car trying to get away from him. Once I got home, I was too scared to even call the police because I thought they would not believe me or blame me because I went over there. I was also too afraid to tell Isaac because he would blame me, then say that I cheated on him, so I kept it to myself.

Well, the next day, Joseph had the nerve to call me like nothing ever happened the night before and that we were still friends. At first, I did not know what to say, but then, I cursed him out and threatened to call the cops or send someone over to his house to kill him; I hung up and never heard from him again. Later that day, Isaac came over. At first, I did not want to say anything, but I told him and believe it or not he seemed upset with me. Isaac honored my wishes and did not do anything and did not call the cops.

Once all this chaos had passed, I had to move on and keep this horrific act to myself. I kept believing that I was not good enough to be in a happy, healthy, and loving relationship. But I would not stop being in relationships. I concluded; I deserved all the bad things that continued to happen to me.

One day, I was out and about, and I ran into my son's father, Michael. I had not seen him for a while. We only dated for a short period before I got pregnant. By this time our son, Malachi, was about 4 years old and he was a very emotional child. My son cried a lot and he loved to suck his fingers to the point where he would have blisters and no matter what I did, I could not get him to stop. When I saw Michael, I did not know how to react since I was nervous, but then we began talking. Michael seemed to be happy to see me. He hugged me and I hugged him back. I instantly asked him if he knew about our son and he said, "yes, why didn't you tell me?" I said, "because I knew you didn't want any kids and I didn't think you would want our child."

At first, it relieved me, and I said, "do you know how old your son is, when is his birthday?" And Michael said, "yes, he's 4 and his birthday is Christmas Day." I looked at him and asked why he never reached out to me, especially if he knew all of this.

Sadly, he did not have a reasonable answer, he just stood there looking clueless. I asked him if he would come to see his son because he needed his father in his life and that he was a very emotional kid. Michael said, "I will come and see him, but what about you and me?" I told him, "there was no you and me, that's how I got into this situation.

I only want you to spend time with your son and get to know him." He said, "okay, I'm going to my mom's house and I will give you her number, call me at 6:00 PM." I believed him and had confidence that he would come to see his son.

Six o'clock came, and I called as he requested. Michael answered the phone and said, "I'm coming but can I spend some time with you too," and I said, "no, like I said before, this is not about you and me anymore, it's about you getting to know your son and spending time with him." He said, "okay, well, call me back at 9:00, I have something to do but I will be there." At nine o'clock, I called Michael and his mother answered. I asked her if he was home and she said no. I told her who I was and that he told me to call him and his mom said, "Sweetie, I don't know where Michael is, but I will tell him you called."

Later that evening, I called again and of course, Michael was still not there. I already knew that he would not be there, and he was not coming to see his son, mainly because I would not give him any sex. So, our son was not his priority and that was the last time I heard from him or ever saw him again. Unfortunately, this hurt me to know that my son would never know his father, because I would not chase down a man who does not want to have anything to do with his child, our child, unless I promised to have sex with him again.

Time had passed and eventually Isaac and I broke up, which probably was the best thing for both of us. Then I met the man I married and now divorced. However, before Darryl and I met, Derrick was back in our daughter's life. He was doing great at being her father and we were doing great as co-parents and friends. He was even spending time with my son, knowing that he was not his.

Derrick finally came to me and wanted us to have a serious relationship. One night, we were together in his mother's basement and for the first time, Derrick asked me to be his girlfriend. At first, I laughed and said, "you don't want me like that, if you just want to continue to have sex, we can still do that, especially since we had a child together." But Derrick said, "no, I'm serious. I really want to be in a relationship with you, I love you." This was what I had been wanting with him ever since I fell in love with him. But because I knew Derrick slept with a lot of women and deep down, I felt he was not serious, I just told him yes and then we made love and I went home. The next few days passed, and I continued to see other guys and that was when I met Darryl.

The way my ex-husband Darryl and I met was kind of bizarre but once we got together, I thought in my heart that he was the best thing for me considering my strong feelings for Reggie. I thought I would not find love ever again in my life and Darryl was the closest thing to it. I was originally dating his cousin William, whom I thought I would have a great relationship with, but he was all about the games and he too did some hurtful things to me. Even after all that, I still tried to give him another chance and to no avail, it did not happen.

In the beginning, I was not anywhere interested in Darryl. William and I, and Darryl and my girlfriend Tammy were all supposed to go out on a double date one Friday evening. The plan was for everyone to meet up together with me. They would ride around with me as I paid my bills and ran some errands, then we would go out. This day was the first day of Darryl and I hanging out together. Because I had my friend Tammy with me, I assumed everything would be fine; how wrong I was.

Endurance is Victory

I was not fully aware that Tammy was so wrapped up in her kids' father and their failing relationship that she was not paying too much attention to Darryl or my car. I had a 1991 Ford Tempo, and my car had the capability where I could leave the car running and take the keys with me as I made errands. This day, I kept the keys with me as I did my running around because I had money in my glove compartment; I had a change caddy under my car seat, and money in my armrest. I had the keys to all of this because I did not want anyone to steal anything from me. Unfortunately, I could not prevent this from happening with three people in my car that I thought I could trust or at least one of them, my girlfriend Tammy.

William said, "why do you keep taking your keys with you, you have us in the car, so you don't need to do that." At first, I was hesitant, then I said, "Tammy, since you're in the car, will you make sure my car is good." She said yes, and William and Darryl both assured me everything would be fine. Again, I was being naïve and stupid, trusting everyone. As the day ended, I checked the money I had leftover to see what I could afford to spend for the night. Lo and behold, all my money was gone, including my change caddy. I was so upset and hurt. Like, how

could they steal from me? Tammy instantly said she really was not paying attention, but she took nothing from me. William and Darryl were
arguing and blaming each other for stealing my money and I did not
know who to believe. I was so upset because that was all I had to last
me until I received my next pay check.

We all were debating for about an hour about who stole my
money because they were the only ones in the car, and it did not just
walk away. William and Darryl both tried to convince me it was not
them. My instinct told me to not believe either of them, but in my heart,
I did not want any trouble, so I just had to believe them and chuck it up
as a loss and needed to be more careful with other people.

Later that evening, William and Darryl connected with me to
convince me they did not steal my money and tried to blame it on
Tammy. However, because I knew her longer than both, I did not
believe them. Deep in my heart, I knew it was one of them, but I could
never prove it. Until this day, I truly believed it was Darryl. I will explain my reasoning later. After they calmed me down, the night
changed and later I ended up with Darryl staying and William leaving

and that was how our relationship began because Darryl never left that night.

In the early part of our relationship, we moved kind of fast. Within 30 days, my car broke down, I lost my job, and it was difficult for me to find another job right away (people now tell me that I had so many red flags, but I did not see any). I was still having guys visit me and call me because I did not know how serious this relationship was. Since the same night we met, Darryl never left, which immediately ended the relationship with his cousin and me. All during this time, I was still having flashbacks to the times I had with Reggie and was still feeling the hurt, but I had to move on.

Within those 30 days after I met Darryl, I became pregnant with my third child. At first, it was devastating news, but Darryl was the first man I had a child with who accepted his responsibility. When I finally came home and told Darryl that I was pregnant, I was expecting him to either leave me or not want to have any dealings or even acknowledge that he got me pregnant like my other children's fathers. Darryl was my first baby father that stuck with me during my whole pregnancy and even after our baby was born.

Our first year was kind of shaky because Darryl could not keep a steady job, but what relationship was not, so I led myself to believe. But what drew me so close to Darryl was that after I told him about my life and my family, immediate and extended, he still loved me and my children and accepted me with all of my flaws and issues, at least I thought that. Also, we went through a lot of tests in the beginning of our relationship that showed me his dedication to us, even though many people did not think so. But the biggest test was when I had to go back down to South Carolina to get my mother, brothers, and sister, because she was not happy there anymore and some of her family members were treating her wrong.

Unfortunately, when I got there, I went to her mother's house and I was so upset and livid at how they were living in her home. My mother and siblings were sleeping in the backroom of her mother's house. I considered this her junk room. I walked in and noticed right away that the room was freezing, dark, and gloomy. They were all sleeping in this bed on top of old clothes, blankets, and whatever else was on that bed. They were surrounded by old furniture and so much junk and only one little kerosene heater to keep them warm in this freezing room.

Immediately, I was fuming and so very disappointed in her mom, supposedly my grandmother Gina. I thought, "how could a mother be so cold and heartless to her own child and grandchildren and feel good about themselves?" With this woman, that was very possible. I came out to the living room and asked her why my mother, brothers, and sister were sleeping in this room like dogs. She said, "this is my house, and she is my daughter, don't you question me how I take care of her, you are the one who asked me to take her." I said to her, "I know I asked you to take care of her, but you are not supposed to treat them like this, you are wrong and you're evil." Well, her mother had this famous saying when someone said something she did not like, "Loose here Satan" and she said it to me. Then I responded back and said to her, "You loose here, Satan, because you have the devil all in you."

Endurance is Victory

I looked at her husband and asked him how could he allow her to treat my mom and siblings like this? The only thing he said was, "All right now, y'all stop that yelling and calm down." That was all he said. I was so disgusted with them both. I told her I was going to take them with me, and she said you are not taking them anywhere and asked me to leave. Unfortunately, because I was alone, I did not know what to do at that moment, so I left and tried to come up with another plan.

The next morning, I was driving back to get my mother and my life changed for the worst, I could have ever imagined. Remember, I said earlier that during my time with Darryl a lot happened, including my car breaking down. Therefore, I needed a car to get my mom and siblings, so I had a friend Thomas, who I also dated, assist me in getting a car because he worked at a car dealership. I really thought he wanted to help me because we were still friends, or so I thought. Thomas loaned me a car from his dealership to help me get my mom Leslie. He had the same type of car that I originally had and told me I would be fine, so I trusted him.

Endurance is Victory

Unfortunately, the South has a way of treating people that are not from the South, especially if you have Northern license plates, as if they think you are doing something illegal. On this morning, I guess being black and a woman, 6 months pregnant, and driving with Pennsylvania license plates, was my fault was. I was driving and out of nowhere I got pulled over by the cops and when he pulled me over, I asked what I had done. He said I ran a stop sign, which I knew was a lie. Then, he asked for my license and registration. I gave them to him and as I waited, suddenly, in a flash, the cop came to me and told me to get out of the car and put my hands behind my back. I asked him what I did, and he said, "they have reported this car stolen."

Immediately, I began singing like a bird. I told him who I was, my family's names on both my mother and father's side, and I even gave them the nickname I truly hated. The cop thought I was some lady from Florida which was where the car was reported stolen from. For the first time in my life, I went to jail for something I did not do and because I trusted another man again.

Instantly, I called my mother and at first, her mother would not let me speak to her. She said, "good for you, that's what you get for coming to get your mom." I said, "it's not my fault, why would you say that to me." Yes, it was painful, but because after all these years, I saw her true colors that proved to me she never really loved me, my mother, or my siblings, but I did not care. I only wanted to talk to my mom and hoped that maybe this time she would help me. So, I spoke to my mom and because she still was not on her medicine because her mom purposely hid it from her, she did not know what to do, no matter how much I pleaded with her.

I asked her if she could help me and she said that Gina still had control of her money. I was crying and begged her for help but because of her mental state, this was not possible. Therefore, I said, "mom, please find your medicine so you can get out of that house, your mom is evil." My mom said, "I am Katrina, but she is hiding my medicine from me and she won't give me my money." I thought how wrong this woman was, but I could not focus on this, I needed to get out of this place.

Endurance is Victory

By this time, in this small town, my family on both sides heard what happened, and the sad part of all this was, none of them had $300 to help pay for my bond to get me out of jail. $300 was a little money, but none of the family on my mother's or father's side could or would come up with the money to get me out, so I spent 30 long crucial days in a room with other women with terrible lifestyles; those use to going back and forth to jail. While in jail, I also met my other little sister on my father's side of the family and a cousin.

Even my uncle on my father's side was locked up on the other side of the jail. My father was in jail in New York, but he found out and started communicating with me. He kept saying "Boo-Boo, what are you doing in there, you're not supposed to be in there." But again, no one could come up with the money to get me out on bond. Back in Philly, I communicated with Darryl and he tried to console me, but it was not helping me. I also spoke with my cousin, Mary, who I also looked up to as an aunt I met on my mother's father's side of the family, and another guy who was a dear friend, and yes, I dated him briefly, but he was a cop and could guide me through all of this. I mean Darryl had been to jail before, he had a record, and I did not; this life was foreign to me.

While in this place, I could not sleep, I was constantly crying, and I would barely eat. I watched a lot of shows with people going to jail and the lifestyle they had to endure, and I was so afraid of being a part of this for something I did not do. As time passed, I had several family members come visit me, but deep down I did not want to see them. I truly felt they were only visiting so they could have something to talk about. My mother did not come to visit me, so I felt I was all alone with my unborn baby.

Miraculously, an attorney, by the name of Bobbi Jean, defended me. I do not know how she was assigned to my case, but she was amazing. Later in life, I found out that my mother hired her, so I guess she did something for me I did not know. I told Bobbi Jean everything that happened, and she said she would do everything to get me out because they were trying to give me 10 years for something I did not do, even though this was my first time in any kind of trouble.

Endurance is Victory

The day of freedom finally came for me. Bobbi Jean struck a deal, and I did not even have to see the judge or sit inside of a courtroom or anything. She told me they were dropping all the charges against me and after a period they would expunge my records. I asked her what this meant, and she said, "yes, you can go home, you are free. It's all over." Next to hearing the cries for the first time of both of my children, this was the next best news ever. Bobbi Jean explained they reported to her that this car was stolen from Philadelphia, Florida, and California by another woman and the police assumed I was that person. However, since I never had a record and I was not the person who stole the car, they let me go free.

Immediately, I went to Aunt Tracy's house and got on the first train back to Philadelphia and I promised myself to never go back to that town for a very long time. Once I arrived back in Philly, back with my other two children and Darryl, that was the first time I felt that he really had my back. He did not leave my kids and run off but stayed at the house to take care of them and my home until I returned; with the help of some of my neighbors.

ANOTHER TRANSITION AND MOUNTAIN IN MY LIFE

During these nine months of Darryl and my relationship, we had a lot of trials, but I thought that this was normal in a relationship with two people who were very different and came from different backgrounds. But when I returned from South Carolina and having that ordeal, none of it mattered to me.

Yes, my mother also had her share of troubles with her sisters and her mother, and even though she treated me the way she did, she still was my mother and I still had to be there for her. Until this day, I can remember my mother telling me how bad some of her sisters treated her and even me when I was a little girl, and we were still living in New York.

I am going to give you a little about the history of my mother's family life. From what I was told by my mother and other family members, my mother was given away when she was little, but no one really knows at what age, because she was out of the family for a long time. Later I discovered that she was given to her great aunt who was on her mother's side of the family. So, for most of my mom's childhood and some of her teenage life, she was not with her family. Then at 16-years-

110

old, my mother ran away from the lady who was taking care of her. Later I found out that this woman was the aunt of my mother's mom, so she was not a stranger. Then this aunt took my mom back to be with her real family, but mysteriously, they had moved to a different location.

Once mom finally located them, her sisters did not seem thrilled to see her at first. I guess because they really did not know her, and she was absent from her family for so long. I mean, can you imagine your mother having three children at first from her first marriage then eight other children from her second marriage and suddenly, a new child pops up out of nowhere and the only one that knows you are your two older sisters? That can be very scary and devastating at the same time, but it never justified their behavior and treatment of her and I.

Well eventually, her sisters and brothers finally accepted her after about two years. She got pregnant with me and that was another shock to the family. Not because my mother was pregnant, but because the child that she had was not the perfect child. I was the child who had a terrible skin disorder and the way her sisters dealt with it was very mean and cruel.

Endurance is Victory

From what I was told by my mother when I was little, some of her sisters used to set me out on the steps with the dog and make me drink my milk with the dog in the winter all because they were afraid of my skin and they did not understand what was going on with me. Then there was one time that my mother told me that one of her sisters threw me down the stairs from the third floor for no apparent reason.

On another occasion, they cut off all my hair to make me look like a boy. I was told they cut up my clothes when people would buy them for me. Also, my family was famous for giving everyone in the family nicknames and mine was Muffin (not a good nickname). For years, I always asked what the meaning was behind this nickname and I was always told that when I younger, I used to hold on to a broom like a baby monkey. Sadly, later I finally found out the real meaning behind the nickname. I will come back to that later in the story. So that put my mother at terrible odds with some of her sisters, even when she got older, especially with her second older sister, Aunt Tracy. The reason I say that was we knew Aunt Tracy for being the "bully" of the family and she always thought that she was the toughest one, even tougher than her younger brothers. So even though Aunt Tracy had been in our life for a very long time, she had her moments where sometimes you did not want to be around her, or she made others fear her. And when my mother moved back down South, that was one moment.

When my mother got sick and moved down South with her mother, it took her longer than normal to get herself together mentally. The reason was because it seemed like her mother had a stronghold over her. I do not know how and why, but she did. But eventually, I talked my mother into getting herself together, not just for her, but for my sister and brothers.

Well, after my mother finally got herself together, she moved back out on her own, but it seemed like her problems got worse, because she let Aunt Tracy and some of her kids move in. Aunt Tracy could help her get herself together, but it seemed like Aunt Tracy took over her house and my mother was feeling scared, like a prisoner in her own house. I took it upon myself again to go down south and get my mother, but this time I went in the middle of the night, drove for about 8 hours, packed up the car, turned right around and brought her back to Philadelphia to get her away from Aunt Tracy. I brought her to live with us for about six months.

Endurance is Victory

At first, everything was fine, but then my mother started treating me like a child in my own home and we just could not get along. This was affecting my relationship with Darryl, because Darryl really could not understand the extent of my mother's issues and mental status until he saw it. But he just could not deal with it. So eventually, I had to tell my mother that it was time for her to move out on her own, because the number one rule was that two women who have two very different personalities and rules of their household cannot live in the same house. Well, my mother did move, and she moved right around the corner from where we lived.

I thought after she moved into her own home, I would have peace. At the time she moved, I took a sabbatical out of the office and became a shuttle driver and then a limousine driver. I was working for a limousine company, where my hours were always so hectic and sometimes, I would work 16 to 18 hours a day, so I stayed gone a lot. When I was not working, I was trying to get as much rest as I could. I had an older neighbor, named Mr. Rob, who was always up when I would leave to go on a run. One morning, he approached me as he normally would with a greeting. Mr. Rob said, "hey baby, I know I get up early, but your mom is over at your house every morning." I looked at Mr. Rob with disbelief and at first, I thought he was joking. I said, "Mr. Rob, stop playing, my mom is not at my house every morning." He said, "yes, she is. Every morning I come outside, I see her either coming to your house or leaving your house with her shopping cart full of clothes."

After I heard this information, I waited until later that day to confront my mom about this information. I called my mom and asked her about it, and she confirmed the information to be true. Later, I asked Darryl if he know about this and he had no clue because the washer and dryer were downstairs, and our bedrooms were upstairs where we closed the doors at night and could not hear anything. With my hearing problem, when extremely tired, I slept on my good ear and could not hear anything. Once I knew about this, I immediately took my key away from my mom. I gave it to her to have in case she needed it in the event of an emergency and coming into my house to wash clothes at all times of the night was not an emergency.

Living life in the projects has its ups and some downs. I remember having an issue with my neighbor Felicia, I believe, simply because she did not like me. We used to always argue about some of the pettiest things. She would always tell me how stupid I was to be with a guy who was not able to take care of me and was using me, and I was so stupid to not see it. I used to always tell her she was just jealous. There was one occasion, where her youngest daughter was outside, and she picked up an old coke can and drank from it.

Being the parent I am, I took the can from the little girl. Felicia came outside when she saw this and assumed, I did something bad to her. I tried to explain to her what occurred, and she did not want to hear it. She caused a big disturbance outside and wanted to fight me. I called my mom and she instantly came over to calm me down. Darryl was not home, so I reached out to him and told him she had a baseball bat and that she busted my car windows to provoke me and made me come outside to fight her. I was not the person to fight, especially since I had kids of my own and that just was not me, but I knew I had to protect my children from this crazy woman over a misunderstanding. Eventually, Darryl, his brothers and cousins showed up to help me and diffused the situation. After all of that, I broke all communication with the neighbor and I focused on my family.

Endurance is Victory

Once Darryl almost made me lose my job with the limousine company. He had a dangerous habit of taking my car without my knowledge or permission. With the limousine cars, I strictly told him that these cars were off-limits, no matter what, but of course, as usual Darryl did not listen to me. When I first got hired with this company, we were told that should anything ever happen to the cars, we would have to pay one million dollars as our liability with the insurance company. Knowing this, I did not have that type of money to give anyway, so I had to be extremely careful.

This day, I had a long night out of state, and I came home to get some sleep. I told Darryl to not take the car and he promised he would not. Unfortunately, I woke up approximately an hour before I should have looked outside, and the car was gone. I was so livid and upset with Darryl, all I saw was red. I called everyone I could think of where he would go, and everyone kept saying he just left. The dispatch was calling me because now I was late picking up my passenger at the airport. I kept giving them every excuse I could to hold them off until he brought the car back. An hour later, I was standing in the middle of the street, crying, nervous, and fuming at Darryl. He finally pulled up and with a big smile, like nothing was wrong. I instantly went off on him, telling him I may lose my job because of what he did. The only thing Darryl said, "I thought you had to go out later, I didn't know." I took the keys and left the house immediately, because I did not know what I might do to him. I was so worried I would lose my job, but I was fortunate. After that fiasco, I could hide it from my supervisor and could keep my job because I was the only one working and I needed this job.

After about eight years of us living in public housing, we had to leave. Not because we wanted to, but because we were behind on our rent because of only one income coming in the house. Darryl seemed to not be able to hold on to a steady job. We had a rough time for a little while until we found another place to live. Then, time went on and we had to leave our second home and that meant that I had to move in with my mom until we found somewhere else to stay. At first, it was okay but after a while it was time for me to move on, because my mother finally came clean and told me the truth about somethings that happened in my life. Some were very painful to hear, but I guess she felt she needed to tell me in her way. I do not know if she did it to hurt me or to just let me know, but either way, it was hurtful.

One thing my mother told me was that after all these years, Greg never even went to jail like I thought he did and like she constantly reminded me he did. He only served five years' probation because it was his first offense and he was in the military, and not five years in jail like I was told for so long. I started thinking, how she could lie to me after all these years, telling me he was in jail when he never served one day? Then, I started feeling betrayed again by my mother, because I was never ever told the truth until eleven years later.

I also could not deal with how every time I turned around, my mother was putting Fred up on this pedestal to my little brothers, like he was this great man. Afterwards, I grew tired of hearing this and was told this devastating news. I hurried back out of my mothers' house because I could not take it anymore.

I understood that my mother had a mental disease and to some, that is partly the answers to the way she was treating me and the things that have happened to me over the years of my life, but for my mother to keep this secret from me that Sheila's father was also our first cousin, was very disturbing; and that she knew, really threw me off.

Well, after that happened, I had to get my thoughts together, but I tried hard not to let all this affect me. After we moved into our new home, I started not wanting to be with Darryl anymore because I could not deal with his job situation and him not being a good husband and father. Me, being the person I was, I did not think that I should have had to continue to deal with someone not working and I was the only one working and not being the man, I thought he would be for our family. I was also listening to other people's opinions, which had an enormous influence on my decision.

Unfortunately, because I constantly told him how unhappy I was and why he did not seem to care, I made the choice to cheat on him. Shockingly, Darryl got a job, but by then I had dealt with all I could, and I did not want him anymore. I was not sure that he would be able to ever support his family financially. Finally, Darryl and I broke up, and again I was on my own with three children, even though deep down, I really did not want to be apart from Darryl. Remember we had about eight years of history and one child together and he was trying to be a father to two other children that were not his.

After Darryl and I broke up, it forced me to move out of the place that we were living in because of my financial situation. Again, I had to move, but this time, I refused to go back to my mother's house. My cousin Iesha was still living in the city, so I asked her if the kids and I could move in with her until I got back on my feet. Well, out of all the people in the world, if I could not trust anyone else, I could trust my favorite cousin Iesha, because remember, we had been through everything together from our early childhood until we became adults. At first, when I moved in with Iesha, I thought everything was fine. Well, I found out how very true that was not. Once we moved in with my cousin Iesha everything about her just transformed. My cousin's brother was also living with her and that was when our relationship unravelled quickly.

Iesha made plans to leave town on a trip to New York for the weekend. When she left, I was not aware until later that she left her brother to be a spy for her against me as if I was some criminal or a stranger. Before Iesha left, I asked her if it was okay if Darryl came to visit and maybe even spend the night with the children and she agreed.

So, I thought everything would be okay; how wrong I was. Once Iesha came back from her trip, she cussed me out for having Darryl there, even after she said it was okay. Then my children were being accused of doing things they did not do. Then knowing that I was trying to save money, so I could move and get back on my feet, she asked for more money. Iesha called me on my job and asked me if I could give her more money that I did not have because according to her, the landlord found out that I was there and needed more money.

Later, I found out that it was not true, so I got my children and went somewhere else until I found another place to live. Even though I had a lot of friends (I had even gotten back in contact with my best friend Benita), I went back to my mom's house just so I could get away from my cousin.

Once I moved out of Iesha's house, she really could express how she truly felt about me after all these years. She first accused my children of stealing something that they did not take. Then she downgraded my children because they did not have fancy clothes and expensive toys like her children because she considered that her and her children were better than we were. And if that was not bad enough, she even went on to degrade me about my skin and how she never liked to hang out with me because of my looks. She even said how she never liked me sleeping in her bed because she thought I was contagious. She went on to say that her husband was better than mine, even though he was on drugs. But he had a better job and paid the bills, unlike my husband, who could never keep a job and was unable to pay any bills.

Once Iesha told me her genuine feelings, I cut all ties with her and I did not want to see her again which was very unfortunate since our children were so close, but I never stopped their relationship. If I thought that I had anyone in my corner, no matter what, it would have been be my cousin Iesha. eventually I had to find out the hard way that her personality was just like her mother's in her own little way. But I would not be like my mother and be afraid of her, because I was told a long time ago that you can still love your family from afar, but do not be anyone's fool and allow them to treat you unfairly.

So after about eight months of us being apart, Darryl and I got back together. Once Darryl and I got back together, we started working on our relationship, so much to the point that we started talking about marriage. But Darryl told me we would not rush into it, especially after how we ended our relationship the first time. After time had passed, we were moving again to another side of town, where there was a big rooming house for various families to live in, preferably single men and women with one or two children. Our family was the largest family in this house.

After time had passed, I received a call from DHS (Department of Human Services) saying that they brought another complaint against me for child abuse and neglect. I was very shocked to hear this. Darryl kept saying that it was my mother. When DHS came to the house, the lady asked the other house guests who did the furniture belong to and they informed them it was mine, along with the dishes, pots, and silverware. After the DHS worker did their investigation for the third time, they apologized to me and said, "we will not bother you and your kids again; if we get another call, we will not follow through."

Unfortunately, later my mother finally owned up to it after Benita confirmed it. Once she left the department, she was able to tell me the truth. As for Darryl and me, by then we were making plans for us to get married. The plans were coming along, and I called everyone to tell them about the big day, especially my family in South Carolina. Benita and I were planning my wedding. She asked me if I was truly ready to get married and I hesitated, but I said yes. I became more and more excited each day, especially up to the day of the event.

Well, on March 15, 2003, the day I thought nothing could spoil my special day for me; again, I was wrong. The morning of my wedding day, I was planning to get ready. While I was prepping myself, I was double-checking the guest list to see if certain special people in my life were going to attend this special occasion.

As the day went on, my girlfriend, Benita, kept telling me to calm down, do not worry about anything, reminding me this was my day. But with the life that I lived, it was kind of hard not to worry. And as usual, I was right. My mother had planned for me to ride in a limo, but the limo originally was supposed to take her and my brothers to the destination where I was getting married. Once the limo arrived, I asked if they had picked my mother up and their response was, "no we didn't." So, I became anxious and Benita and everyone else comforted me and kept reminding me that I should not worry about anything. Well, once we arrived at the hall and I got into the lobby, I saw my beautiful sister Sheila sitting there waiting for me to come in. Sheila's first question was, "where is mommy, she is not here" and I said, "I don't know maybe she is on her way." Then Sheila said, "let's call her, she has a cell phone," but I told her, "no, we will wait." Deep down inside, I was really hurting because out of all the times that she did not show up to anything important in my life, I figured she would not miss the most important day of my life.

Well, as the ceremony began, I was still looking around for a second, until I looked into the eyes of Darryl and I saw the tears streaming down his face and during that moment I became so wrapped up in him, I forgot about everything that was happening.

After the ceremony was over, I figured she came, as she would not miss this. Well, again I was wrong. A girl's most precious day of her life, her wedding day, my mother did not even show up. As I was being greeted by my aunts and my grandmother from my father's side, I became very disappointed, but they all tried to encourage me, including my father. Deep down inside no one knew how truly hurt and devastated I was, except my girlfriend, Benita. Another important event and Leslie chose not to be there to support her oldest child. At the end of all the festivities, as everyone was leaving, I expressed to one of my aunts how I felt about my mother not showing up and Benita came over and said to me, "are you upset because your mother did not show or are you happy because your father's here, now which one really matters?" I took only a second to think about that and said, "you're right, my dad came all the way to Philly from Georgia, and he didn't have to do that."

After everything was over, our life began as one extended family, and do not think for one second it was all a bed of roses. But I waited until about three weeks before I finally spoke to my mother and when we talked, the first question that I asked was, "why did you not come? what happened, why did you not let my brothers come?" And you know what her response was, "I don't want to talk about it now; don't bother me with this right now." After my mother said this to me, my heart just dropped, I did not know what to say and I felt even more distraught when I talked to her than how I felt the day of the wedding and she was not there. Again, more questions added to the other questions in my life that I will never get answers to. Because they taught me, I must always respect my mother and father. At that moment I had to catch myself and not say anything ignorant or disrespectful. Well, eventually being the person who I am, of course, I ended up still communicating with my mother, but I never spoke to her again about my wedding. So, she has never seen my wedding pictures even to this day.

More time had passed, and I thought about relocating out of Philly because the cost of living had become unbearable, along with crime. I was afraid for my children, not knowing whether they would be alive from one day to the next. It was mainly for Darryl that I wanted to move because we were struggling badly. Our rent was getting ready to increase again and Darryl seemed to be oblivious to everything or he did not care or was not paying attention. I was the main one paying all the bills. I asked Darryl, "how can I help you be better," and he said, "I don't know, maybe I need a change of scenery, maybe I have done too much in Philly."

Being the wife I was, I listened, and made plans for us to move to help him and help our family, so I thought. I called my father and told him I wanted to leave but I did not want to move to the country, Darlington, SC. So, he told me to take a visit for a short time to where he was living in Augusta, Georgia. Well, my family and I planned for this trip. Once we took the trip to Georgia, my husband and I were very pleased with what we had seen and experienced. While I was going back and forth to prepare our family for the move, I realized that not only was my mother mentally disturbed, but my father was as well.

The reason I said this was, I finally could see the other side of my father that my sisters were telling me about, like some of his personality. I guess because I was so wrapped up in the idea of my dad being this "good man", he would do nothing to me, because he knew what I had been through. And, because he was not a part of my life until I was 21 years old, I was still in Daddy's little girl mode.

Well, how wrong I was. As I was preparing our family to move to Georgia, I had to take several trips to get everything in order. One time when I took the trip to Georgia, I got into a jam and the one key person I thought I could depend on was my dad. I called him and told him my situation. He then instructed me to stay with a family member, the one I had never met in Charlotte, NC, and he would get me the next day. This family member kept trying to warn me that my father was not the man I thought he was, and I would see. She even tried to convince me to just go back to Philly, but as usual, I would not listen. I tried to give him the benefit of the doubt. The next day came and that is when my eyes opened to his personality. The family member dropped me off where he was in Shelby, NC. At first, I thought it was a bad idea, but I went anyway. I mean, I became stranded and I believed he could help.

At first, everything seemed okay, then my dad did a 180 degree turn on me. He kept asking me the same questions like, "why are you here? where is your man? why would you come down here without enough money?" Each time I gave the same answer. Then he started to bad mouth my husband saying things like, "why can't he send you the money, he is a bum, he is not any good, why won't he be a man?"

And again, I kept explaining myself. Then I got frightened because all of this was happening in front of other so-called family members and no one did anything to stop this. They just sat and watched. Then my dad said that he would not help me, so I called my husband and told him what was going on, and of course, he was furious. Mainly because he could not do anything from Philly.

Then, I tried to find my way back home, even if I had to hitch-hike, but he kept preventing me from doing that and he kept asking me, "why are you acting like this?" Now, go figure, I am the one stranded and came to him for help and he just turned on me like I was a stranger. I was so afraid of him and everyone in the house. I walked outside and began trying to walk down this dark, scary road back to the city in order to get help from anyone and just get away from these people who I thought were my family, but mainly my father.

He ran behind me and grabbed my arm hard. He kept hollering and yelling at me and calling me names. He started talking about my choices in a man and became very violent. He said, "why are you being so stupid, you can't walk down this dark road by yourself." I said, "well, I don't care." As long as I did not have to be near him, I didn't care. I asked, "why are you treating me like this, what did I do for you to change and treat me so badly?" He never answered and dragged me back into the house. The entire time the family watched the whole scene and did nothing to help me.

Finally, I survived the next morning and one of the family members graciously offered to help me get back home. He asked me how much it was that I needed, and I told him. Then he took me to his church for help. After this incident, it really opened my eyes to whom I could really trust and who I could not. I guess because I thought he was my father, not considering that I never knew him my entire childhood and part of my adult life and the fact that people can change.

Once I finally got back home safe and sound, I vowed I would not speak to my father for a while. Now I would have to treat him like a stranger, especially because it seemed like my grandmother, his mother, became upset with me without even knowing what had happened or caring to know what happened because he was her son. Until this day, I think she treated me this way because of whatever my father told her to make himself look good. I was even told later by a family member that I stayed with that my father had everyone thinking that I was a drug addict and that I could not be trusted with money, even though it was my ex-husband Darryl.

After I found all of this out, I told one of my sisters and my mother about what happened, and of course, my mother said, "I told you he was crazy." Even my sister said that was why she treats him the way she did because of his personality. For a while, I did not call him.

Even my husband despised him but because I had not really known the man and I still loved him, I eventually started communicating with him again. I also started doing some background checks on his life to understand why he acted the way he did, and I found out that he was just like my mother, dealing with schizophrenia. Again, I must let bygones be bygones because as the Bible says, "honor thy father and thy mother that thy days may be long on earth."

LIFE IN ANOTHER STATE GAVE MORE LESSONS

In November 2004, I had made my mind up that we had to leave for the survival of our family. Deep down, I think Darryl did not truly know how serious I was until I put my plan into action. I told our friends and family that we were moving. Of course, no one believed us, especially Darryl. Everyone kept saying, "he's never leaving Philly" and I said, "yes, he will, he said he is ready." Looking back at it now, I guess everyone knew better than I did. I started my search for a new location in the south. I knew I did not want to move to Darlington because that location was too small and slow for a city girl like me. Almost all my family on both sides lived there, and I did not want to be too close to any of them.

Then one day, I told Darryl that I found a place for us to move to. Of course, he said, "why don't we wait until the next income tax check to do this?" I became very frustrated and disappointed in him because he was not on board. I told Darryl, "no, I'm not doing that again, we keep waiting and nothing is getting better with you." So, I continued working on my plans without his help. Finally, I was ready to leave. I had my kids and a couple of neighbors help me pack up the house and put everything into storage. You wonder what Darryl was doing, he was sleeping and did not get up to help with anything.

The only thing that was left in the house was the mattress and box spring we slept on. I went upstairs, woke Darryl up and told him to get up so I could move the bed. He jumped up and said, "what are you talking about, I thought we were going to wait until income tax." I said, "no, get up, I found us a place and we are leaving." Darryl laughed and said, "you're crazy" and laid back down. I said, "Darryl, please get up, your mom helped us with a rental car and I only need to put this bed in storage, everything is packed and gone." He looked at me in shock, looked around the house, and said, "damn, you are serious, okay I will go if you give me $20." I laughed and looked at him like he was crazy.

Unfortunately, Darryl liked to smoke marijuana and drink heavily. So, I told him that he could not drive that far if he was high. He said, "I won't, just give me the $20 and I will leave with you, I'm serious." I was thinking, as I usually do, anything to keep my man happy in this car. I gave Darryl the $20, he left, came back, and said he was ready to move with a big smile on his face. Yes, after years later, I know how it sounds that I had to pay my husband to move with me for a better life. Again, so I thought it would be.

My family eventually moved to Augusta, Georgia, in November 2004 after all the roadblocks. I became determined to help my ex-husband become a better man, father, and husband for our family. Unfortunately, we moved, and life gave me a whole different ballgame of lessons. Upon arriving in Augusta, I will honestly say I did not do my proper research and homework on this town. On the surface, when my ex-husband and I first visited, I thought this was a great place and maybe we could have a fresh start with a lot of options as we did in Philly, just in a country town.

How very wrong I was. On my first job in Augusta, I was only making $8.50 an hour, and you are probably wondering what was wrong with that. Well before we moved from Philly, I was making $16.00 an hour. Then, my ex-husband could only get a job making $5.15 an hour, which was even worse. Together, the struggle really became real for me and my family. I was thinking to myself, why did I move, what a mistake I made, and now, I was stuck. Once arriving in Augusta, we were planning to move into our own home.

Unfortunately, once the owners realized we were African American, they decided that the home was no longer available. Since I did not have a backup plan, we stayed in a hotel for a couple of weeks, because I did not want to bother my dad's girlfriend about a place to stay. However, my money ran out. I had to come up with another plan and I called my dad and asked for help, which I truly regretted after the way he treated me. But I had to think about my children and their needs. He contacted his girlfriend and convinced her to let us stay with her. At first, I was totally against it, but we did not have a choice since I did not know anyone in this town, and we had no more money.

We stayed with Shelly for a few weeks, which felt like months. At first, she seemed to be very nice, but her true colors came out quickly. Shelly had a dog that shed hair like crazy, which I was allergic to and the kids also had some type of allergic reaction. I kept telling her that the dog would not stop scratching, and something was wrong, but she would not listen.

One day, this church came around the neighborhood to get everyone to come and the incentive was that they would give everyone in the house $20. You must be thinking why a church would do this and I thought the same thing, but our monies were low, and we all needed the help. We all went to church, even Darryl. For as long as when we were together in Philly, I could never get him to go to church with me. He would go to the Jehovah's Witness hall with his mother and that was only because he was always going to her for help and she said that he had to go to the hall. Of course, I was against that because of my Christian beliefs, and I still had flashbacks of the lady who raised my mother forcing me to go to the hall. I got Darryl to go to church so we could get some extra money in our pockets.

After we left the church, my kids told me that Shelly took their money. This made me highly upset but I was afraid to confront her because we were living in her house. I have always learned, when you're living under someone else's roof, adult or not, you can't cause too much friction, because you are in their house. Therefore, I had to work on finding us another place quickly. Unfortunately, we ended up staying in a shelter at the Salvation Army. This was my breaking point. I was looking at my ex-husband like, "why can't you help us and prevent this from happening?" This to me was a sign that maybe I should not have stayed in this town, but I had no more monies until the next income tax time, so we were stuck.

We stayed in this shelter for about two days and the shelter graciously helped us find our first place. It was a one-bedroom apartment that we all shared. As a family of five, my kids slept in the bedroom and my ex-husband and I slept in the living room. In my eyes, it was a roof over our head, until I could do better. I got a job that had me commuting very far from home to work.

Unfortunately, I did not do my proper research on Augusta, as I thought I had. They had limited public transportation; the bus system only ran every 30 minutes during peak hours and every hour during off-peak hours. Which meant, I had to find transportation back and forth to work. Because Darryl was only working for minimum wage of $5.15 an hour and not full time, so we did not have enough monies for a car or taxi rides. Therefore, I would walk to work, which was equivalent to a 30-minute ride. Every morning, I would get up at 4:30 and walk at least an hour to work.

I was from the city and did not know anyone here and was embarrassed to ask anyone for a ride to work at first. Then, I became friendly with one or two people and would ask for a ride back home. For about a week or two, I would do this without Darryl knowing of my day-to-day routine.

Finally, after a month, he woke up one morning and asked when my ride would show up to take me to work. I told him to go back to sleep, they should be here shortly. He refused, so I finally told him what I was doing.

At first, I thought, my husband was finally going to step up to the plate and take care of his wife. Right? Wrong! He paid for a taxi for a week, then told me to ask for rides from people at my job. By now, it was income tax time again, so I thought I could get myself a car and everything would be better.

It took me about a few days of walking or taking cabs to different dealers, trying to get a reliable vehicle for my family. One dealership almost approved me but when he found out I was from Philadelphia, he said, "how do we know you won't get this car and go back to Philadelphia and not make your payments." I said to him, "I moved my entire family here, I have no savings and no additional income, how will I get there?" Unfortunately, he denied me the vehicle. By the grace of God, I finally found a dealer who would give me a chance.

Endurance is Victory

After a few years of staying in Augusta, GA, life for me kept hurling lessons, rocks and putting walls around me, I had never faced as an adult with kids. Darryl still could not seem to get his life together and be the parent, husband, and provider I needed him to be. Our struggles got worse by the moment. Over time, Darryl became worse and worse. His attitude was mean, angry, sometimes happy, sometimes sad, confusing, and disappointing. Then, I started realizing my money started disappearing more than it did in Philly. I had to start hiding my money and even change bank card information because somehow, he got my PIN and was taking money from my bank account.

Unfortunately, Darryl had a terrible drinking and narcotics habit to the point where, if he did not have these items, the house would not be happy until he got them. I only thought it was marijuana and liquor. Over the years, people kept asking if he was on anything harder and I always would say, "not that I know." Their response would always be that marijuana does not make a person act like he was acting. I was very naïve to that lifestyle. I drank alcohol, but it never altered my behavior or personality as it did Darryl's. Even when I would express my frustration and disappointment to Darryl, he would listen for a minute, then go back to his old ways. Unfortunately, because of my dissatisfaction in our marriage, I was unfaithful. I was not proud of it, but I could not seem to get through to him, even when I confessed to doing it. I was hoping it would affect him to make him change, so he would not lose his family, but it made no impact.

My breaking point started in 2009, but it took me much longer finally to close this chapter. I finally had gotten a job that I thought would be a sustainable one, a place where I could have stability and retire. After working my first job in 2004, I lost the job because the contract abruptly ended. I began as a contractor for the largest state hospital/school in Augusta. Finally, I became permanent in 2006, which was a dream for me to begin my chapter of success, stability, longevity, and prosperity. They employed me at the city's state hospital/college Medical College of Georgia in the Student Affairs office of the School of Nursing. For the first three years of steady employment at this institute, I thought everything was looking up, even though Darryl still could not get himself together. My focus was only on the health and welfare of my kids and Darryl, because he was still my husband, and the bills still needed to be paid. Our financial situation had gotten so bad, from Darryl's stealing from me and not being able to hold down a steady job, but always wanting his habits fulfilled. I had ten payday loans at one time just to keep my head above water with rent, car note, utilities, and the children their needs while still trying to have some type of peace in life.

For some time, a lot of my co-workers always kept telling me how racist my supervisor was, but I refused to believe or accept it until it was blatantly in my face. However, for the first time in history, a black man was elected for President of the United States. This was something that generations before me thought would never happen. I even thought it would never happen, but God opened the door for it to happen. During the campaign of President Barack Obama, my supervisor and her supervisor showed their true colors. It first began when I told my supervisor early on that I was going back to school to further my education so I can advance my career.

Endurance is Victory

My other co-workers were seeing things for what they were and were moving into other positions. Because my income was limited to me being the main breadwinner, my wardrobe was not always up to par. So, my supervisor came into my office one day and asked me why I was I trying to leave her department. I told her I felt that I had exhausted this role and was looking to advance myself into something different. She looked at me and said, "well, you're never going to be better, with the clothes you're wearing. You should go to the Salvation Army, Goodwill, or Walmart to get better clothing. Why do you want to leave me, everyone that works for me wants to leave?"

First, it shocked me that she was saying this to me. She knew my situation and that I only made $12.50 an hour and with three kids and a husband, who could not be a good provider. She signed my timesheet every week, so she knew my income. I said to her, "as soon as I'm able to, I will work on my wardrobe, as for why people keep leaving, I cannot answer for them, I just want to advance my career, that's why I was going back to school."

Endurance is Victory

After this dialogue with my supervisor, I was very shocked. Despite that, I thought about what others told me. Then things kept getting worse. Every time I kept applying for other positions, I was close, but never chosen without a reasonable explanation. Someone was kind enough later to tell me that my supervisor Pam was blocking any position I applied for, so I would not leave and to keep my eyes open and watch myself.

During this time, more and more things kept occurring. I remember Pam asking me why when she visited schools to introduce the diversity program and would tell the kids that her dream home was a double-wide trailer, Black kids would not pay any attention to her. I informed her that she could not relate to their reality. She did not currently live in a trailer and her car was not less than, so they would not understand. She said, "that's why we had the African doctor to tell his story, he was just like them too." I said, "he's from Africa, he probably makes more than you and those kids and he's not from our country, so he is not like us." She looked and acted confused. As time passed, because I was the only person in the Student Affairs Department left, our department merged with the Faculty Affairs, so we could use their personnel resources. At first, I was thinking this was great, well I was wrong.

Eventually, a co-worker blessed me with better clothing that enhanced my wardrobe from one of her family members who wanted to donate, and she thought of me and my situation. I was so very grateful and humbled that this person would want to give me such nice clothes. Pam saw this and was shocked, so she told me she had some clothes for me as well. I told her I would not need them and thanked her. Around this time, it was time for us to plan our convocation for students. Pam called one evening to ask me what I was wearing, I told her probably a black skirt and a cute blouse.

I did not think of it as anything wrong, well I was wrong. She stated she had a lime green jacket with black buttons that she was going to give me. My thoughts were that it would be cute, and I would accept that. Once I arrived at work the next morning my co-worker said Pam had said that she left a bag for me because I had nothing to wear. I looked at her and thought she was joking. So, I looked in the bag and showed her. It was the jacket that she and I talked about. I told her about our conversation to clear up any misunderstandings. Later, Pam said that she brought in a suitcase and told me it had clothes in there for me and that I should come to her car to retrieve it. I told her, "no, thank you." So, days later, she placed the bag in my office. My daughter came to visit me. We looked in the bag and I placed the suitcase back in her office. These clothes looked ancient and were not my new style of taste.

Now that our department had limited personnel resources, I was told that I always had to be at work. However, a co-worker who was White, could leave work without notice or work from home when faculty really needed her onsite. Then, the most shocking thing occurred that affected me more than I knew. My other supervisor, Jane, came into the office and said to me and my co-worker, who was also Black, "y'all not going anywhere, how do those shackles feel on you, are they tight, you not leaving us."

My co-worker and I looked at each other in shock and anger. We both asked, "did she really say that?" My co-worker said, "I know I must leave this department" and I said, "I'm working on it hard now."

Endurance is Victory

Jane made this statement every day for at least two weeks. Then she would come in and say, "my new President, John McCain/Sarah Palin sounds so good, I can't wait for them to run our country." Again, we would say nothing, only look at each other in disappointment.

For me, what broke the camel's back was when my son's school called to tell me he was sick, and I had to pick him up. Pam said that I could not leave, or I would get reprimanded. I told her the school kept calling me, but she would not let me leave. I could not afford to lose my job, so I had to tell the school I could not come. I was so hurt, frustrated, and angry, but there was nothing I could do. However, the White co-worker Linda could do whatever she wanted with no repercussions. Ever since I moved to Augusta, many people told me I had to play the game, be a part of the "Good Ol' Boy" system to live and survive here as a black person, especially because I was not from here.

To me, this mentality made little sense when the racism was so in your face and you basically had to do what "The Massa" (Master) said or you would lose your job. They also informed me that I was in an At-Will State, meaning that any company could fire you with no probable cause. You could look wrong, smell wrong, the management could have a bad day, and they could end your employment. However, in my mind, I thought that was not fair to hard-working people, especially in the black community where you are basically at their mercy for your livelihood.

After this treatment at work, I ended up going to the EEOC department to file a formal complaint. Then, my nightmare at work became ten times worse. Immediately, I received a write up saying that my performance at work was not up to par. Mind you, I had been working at this place for three years with no issues, no complaints.

The Dean, Lucille and my supervisor were always raving about me to where the Dean wanted me to work for her. But my supervisor Pam fought hard to keep me with her instead. Then Pam commented and said, "if it wasn't for me, you wouldn't be here, I molded and groomed you to be what you are, and I need you to be here to relate to your people." Another shocking comment and I thought to myself, "no, I'm here because you know I am a good, loyal employee, and no one else would stay to work for you. I walked in already molded, that is why you fought to keep me in your department. You had nothing to do with any of that, and I can relate to my people unless they are my family, every black person isn't the same."

Within this department, the comments kept hurling after I made the complaint against my supervisor and I felt stuck in this place they called work. At this institute, every year they would do a Martin Luther King Jr. celebration to celebrate his legacy between them and Paine College.

This year, the jabs kept coming. I was at the ceremony celebrating and enjoying the performance, like everyone else. Jane, my other supervisor came back to the office and said, "Katrina are you ok?" I was like, "yes, why?" Then she said, "well, I saw you clapping and being extra excited at the ceremony, I thought something was wrong." I said, "I was doing the same as everyone else, I don't see any issues." After I said that, Jane walked away laughing.

By now, the USA has its first Black President, President Barack Obama. The entire building was silenced, so quiet you can hear a pin drop and crash. No one would say anything. They informed us we could not post any pictures in our office at all. I posted mine inside my cabinet, so if you looked in the cabinet you would see them. Next, who walked in the door, Jane, and she said, "Katrina, did you get that call?" I said, "no, did a student or faculty member call?" She said, "no, did you get the call from Obama, I hear he is looking for good people." I respond with, "no, but if he calls, I will be the first to help any way I can." I gave her a big smile, looked, and walked away. On this day, nothing anyone said could break me. Our culture had our first own Black President who represented our community and culture.

Later, I went back to EEOC to provide these additional details, along with other documentation to support my claims. At the end of all this, both Jane and Pam were sent to diversity training and given a slap on the hand. There was an acknowledgement of racism and retaliation for reporting the offense. The office environment was very unbearable and tense for me. I was receiving weekly reports that I was not performing in my role, which were false. Then monthly reports, showing the same, which would be documentation for them to end my stay.

Endurance is Victory

On September 9, 2009, the date after I returned from my birthday weekend, my employment formally ended. The tricky way they played it was that Friday. I came to work and did not have any access to my computer or the system.

I also had a background in IT and already had been given the heads up from a co-worker. I already had a feeling that this was going to happen, I just did not know when and how they would play it out. The director of Human Resources came to talk to me and informed me that Pam had reported that I left my workspace without permission or notification to any of my co-workers.

This was very inaccurate information. In the days before my personal laptop needed some work. You are probably wondering why I was taking my personal laptop to work. There was an instance when our network was down and I could not operate my work desktop, so they instructed me to bring my personal laptop to work because grades were due at the end of the semester and I handled this process.

Therefore, I could bring my personal laptop to work for troubleshooting, if needed. On this day, I informed my supervisor Pam and my co-worker Debra of this situation. They both knew of my whereabouts and had my contact number. During all this chaos and investigation from EEOC, my supervisor was not coming in the office and only communicated with me via phone calls or emails.

I let my guard down, and they used this opportunity to end my employment. This was a devastating blow to my heart and my income. Now I was unemployed and was living in a state where unemployment was only $200 a week, which was not enough for my family and me to survive on. Unfortunately, because this was a "Good Ol Boy" company that wholeheartedly practiced in their system, they blocked my unemployment, and I was now left with no income.

Darryl once again lost yet another job and I had to find another job immediately. While I was on this journey, I also sued the institute. Eventually, I found other employment while going through this process. The result was not what I expected; the process ended and a mediator settling the case, because they fought as a private institution. The satisfaction was that everything they had done and put me through was all in black and white, and for me, I had to settle with that outcome.

Later before I left Augusta, I did run into my co-worker Debra and she tried to apologize for not helping me during that situation. She said, "I wanted to, but they said they would fire me." I said, "you didn't think about what they did to me was wrong and how it affected my family?" Debra said, "yes, well Pam did ask if I wouldn't mind having you back." I told Debra, I would not go back for anything in the world, my name and reputation was tarnished because of their actions, and I would be a fool to go back to that racist place. I began employment with another company, and yet again, I lost another job not because of my actions but because of the company.

After this, I gained employment with another company. I stayed at this place of employment for two years, and again it ended because by this time, I was frustrated with this town, Darryl, and my had chosen to uproot my family to this town. For the first time in my career, I had lost four jobs within five years.

In 2011, I had gotten so frustrated with Darryl; I had asked him again to leave because in my heart our relationship was over once more. Then, once more he convinced me to take him back and this time when he came back, he finally admitted to stealing from me. When I asked him why, he said, "I needed money and you wouldn't give it to me." I said, "I didn't give it to you because we needed it for the house, but I always still provided for your needs and you stole from your family."

He tried to convince me of his actions, but I did not listen and was going to start over again. Until this day, I feel that I should have left Darryl in Philly because at one time, he told me he did not believe he was the man I needed because he could not give me what I needed. However, being the woman I was, and as hard-headed as I was, I saw more potential in him than he could see in himself and I decided to still fight for us. But, if I did not go through the experiences I did, I would not be able to share my story.

I gave Darryl another chance, and this time, I had expectations I needed from him and for this marriage to work. For the first three months it started out well, then when we moved to another place, I saw the old Darryl return, but again, I ignored the signs and kept on course. Fast forward to 2012, before I lost my 4th job, I had to have major surgery, which had me on FMLA for 6-weeks. January 2012 was the year that my life was on the rollercoaster ride to hell and back many times over. While I was home recuperating, I filed my income tax on January 25, 2012 and received a notification from the IRS that my taxes were filed for the year. Well, to my surprise, this information was incorrect. Upon further investigation, I was a victim of Tax Identity Theft and Fraud.

Again, Darryl lost another job and I had to force myself back to work because my first FMLA check was $93 and I could not pay my rent or any other bills with that money. From January to May I had to fight the IRS to prove and convince them I never filed my taxes for the year, and I needed my money, so we would not get evicted. Eventually, I got my income tax refund after they did an audit and realized that I owed additional monies. By this time, I was so backed up on our bills that I was swimming deep in debt and we had to move to another place.

Before our move, I ended up meeting a man name Junior (who I'm with now) and fell deeply in love with him. Out of all the relationships I had, he was the first man concerned about me and my happiness and not just what he was getting out of me sexually. Unfortunately, I had another affair, but I was at a point where I became done with Darryl. Junior and I had this special connection, like no other guy I have ever dated, even different from Brian and myself.

Honestly, I cannot fully describe it, which is why I began calling him my "heart puller." Please, know that Junior is not perfect, he had his flaws and faults but had always been consistent in our bond, our conversations, where we could talk about anything and everything. Nothing was off-limits, without being uncomfortable, and it just seems natural with him. Even when we were out socializing or in a place of business, others could sense our connection and instantly say "you both deserve each other" and we just look at each other and laugh. Junior's and my chemistry are undeniable.

I remembered we were in his house talking about my life and my issues with Darryl, and Junior said; "even if we don't last or this doesn't go anywhere, you deserve someone so much better than him." Junior would ask me, "why did you stay with him for so long." For the first time, honestly, I did not have an answer to this question. I said, "I don't know because I fell out of love with him after I forced myself to fall in love with him from the beginning."

I always loved Darryl, because of our child, but I did not instantly fall in love with him. It took years for this to happen. And to make matters worse, my sister Veronica on my dad's side had passed away on December 8, 2012, because of losing her battle with breast cancer and this was so heart breaking for me. As with some of my other siblings on my dad's side, our relationship was not the strongest because of the division our dad caused between us girls over the years. Veronica and I were a little closer and had experienced a lot when she was still alive.

When my sister passed, I truly saw how hurt my dad was, but he tried very hard to hide it. I can remember we were all at the house during repast and he joked and laughed and was telling jokes about me and my husband Darryl and how he was not good for me, and again, making me look bad in front of everyone. However, because he was grieving, I just overlooked it all.

Endurance is Victory

The next day, Daddy called me laughing and said, "Boo-boo, your daddy shot the tv." I said "what, why did you do that?" He said, "I don't know. I had a dream and then, I woke up and shot the tv." I told him I would be over to see him the next day and check on him. Well, after that visit, I promised I would never be in the same room alone with my dad. That night, we were in the house chilling and talking. Somehow the conversation led to how upset he was about what Greg and Fred had done to me. I told him I was good, it happened, and it was over.

Suddenly daddy wrapped his arm around me to console me, or so I thought. Then the next thing I knew he was trying to place his hand on my breast and said, "I can see why they wanted you." I instantly jumped up and said, "what are you doing? You are my dad." He just laughed and I ran out of the house immediately, crying. I immediately called my other sisters and told them what happened.

One of my sisters just laughed as if it were a joke and I told her I was serious. Since I felt they did not take me seriously, I had to play this off the next day, so I could keep the peace until I went back home.

Endurance is Victory

Mind you, I was used to putting on the game face and I learned to still be around my attacker or anyone who harmed me, so I would not be confrontational. I had to do this with my mom, Greg, and Fred. Unfortunately, I told no one else about this except Junior later in our relationship once we got closer after he had already met him. Which I kind of regretted him meeting my dad, but I was thinking I wanted him to see that I met someone better than Darryl.

On January 4, 2013, I walked outside and found that the only vehicle we had between us had been re-possessed. I walked back inside, and all Darryl did was turn his back against me and asked what the finance company had said. I asked him what he thought they said, they wanted their money, or my car goes to auction. Before they took my car, I had received a call in December, informing me I was a month behind. I planned to make a payment and when I informed Darryl of this arrangement, he laughed and said, "they will do nothing. I said, "yes, they will," but I kept on trying to pay as much as I could.

By this time Darryl had another job, but I never really received any money from him. For the first time with this job, I had to put his name on the lease and on a utility bill, which I did. Over the 17 years, we had been together; I had never put his name on any bills or lease we ever had, because he was not consistent with employment and I was the main breadwinner of the house. Once my car was taken again, I had to ask for help and that was when I was ready to end this relationship for good. After they had taken my car to Atlanta to be ready for auction, I had to find a way to Atlanta to pick up my car, and Darryl did not help with any of this endeavor.

Once I brought the car back, he was glad to jump back in it and ride around town like nothing happened. He said to me, "I know you want me gone, but I will help you pay back the money to get the car." After Darryl promised me, I said, "okay" and again took him for his word. I waited until April and informed Darryl that I was very unhappy; I wanted a divorce and him out of my house for good. At first, he would not listen to me, then for about a month or two he became a different person and tried to change. By this time, I was done with him and all his shenanigans and did not care about him nor was I in love with him any longer. In June 2013, everything ended where he tried to kill me.

Endurance is Victory

All I asked Darryl was to take his name off the water bill, but he refused to do this. So, I went down to the water department, explained my situation and they informed me that if I paid the last bill, they would take his name off. I did this, came home, and told Darryl. I asked if he could give me half of the money back, which was only $40.00 but Darryl said, "did you take the bill out of my name?" I said, "yes," and he said, "then that is all you are getting from me." Instead of me getting upset or loud, I just left the house to clear my head.

Once I returned, Darryl came into my room, because by this time, we were not sleeping in the same bed, and pulled out a butcher knife, and said, "I hate you, I should gut you like a fish." I was scared but then said "whatever." He said, "you're a whore, I never should have married you and I know you're with someone else." I said, "I was a good whore, you married this whore, and you gave this whore a baby and you let this whore take care of you." Darryl slapped me and I instantly called the police. The police came but would not take him away.

So, Darryl tried it again. I asked if he could get off the computer, he would not, so being a little vindictive, I turned the breaker off. He finally got up and said, "all you had to do was ask." I said, "I did." Then, he kept talking and saying nasty things to me and said, "I know who you're in a relationship with, my friend told me." Darryl continued, "I would never be with a woman like you ever again." I responded, "you will never find another woman who would put up with your mess and I promise you, I will never find another man like you ever again in my life." That is when Darryl punched me in the face, but I got away from him, grabbed the knife, and threw it in our daughters' room because she wasn't home.

I then ran out of the house to find the police. Shockingly no cop was in sight and we lived right across the street from a police substation. On this night, it was raining very hard, so I drove directly to the police station to file a report. After explaining to the police what occurred, they went to the house to pick him up and took him to jail.

Once he left, I went home and found that Darryl had another knife under the sofa, which he was sleeping on. I called Junior and told him what happened, and he said, "why didn't you call me, I would have come right over." I said, "no, because if something would have happened, I would have to explain to my daughter why her dad was dead, hurt, or in jail, and I did not want to get anyone else involved in my relationship." Junior said, "I understand, that makes sense." I cleaned up the pieces of my life when Darryl left. Our divorce was granted on October 10, 2013 and my chapter with Darryl had concluded.

A SECOND CHANCE AT PEACE, JOY, AND REFLECTION

Once my chapter with Darryl ended, years later I told Junior that I had to leave Augusta, GA, as there was nothing left there for me. I began feeling depressed; it felt like it overwhelmed me with negative energy all the time. The only happiness and solace I had was when I went to church or when Junior and I were together, which was all the time.

I had too much heartache, less success with my career, and I felt Augusta could not offer me what I needed to succeed. Junior said, "I definitely understand, there's nothing here. If I was not in the situation, trying to rebuild myself, I would leave too." That moment, I felt I could not wait for him or anyone else. I remember telling everyone that I was leaving, and nobody believed me.

Then, one day, someone asked, "where are you going, back to Philly or NY?" I said, "no, that will always be my home, but I want something different." Then, they suggested for me to go to Charlotte, NC. I asked, "what's so special about Charlotte, to me it's the south and just like Augusta." And they said, "no, it's very diverse and you have more options." After hearing this, it sold me. I began taking trips back and forth and instantly, I loved it. It was like this place gave you better energy and positive vibes.

Therefore, on December 31, 2015, I prayed as usual, and began packing. When the new year started, I decided that in 2016, I was moving from Augusta, aka to me (Disgusta, GA), and onward to Charlotte. Before leaving Augusta, GA I did not really have a plan. I knew that if I survived living in Augusta with my children and a husband who was not supportive; I learned a lot and I could survive on my own in a new city with no one. It could not get any worse than when I was living there.

Endurance is Victory

Upon arriving in Charlotte in February 2016, my first aim was to gain this job that I was waiting for, which was also a blessing. That was how I began an amazing job in my field of IT, at a company where I felt valued. However, when I moved here, I had a minor delay in finding residence, so I stayed in hotels at first then found out that I had a family who also lived here, so I stayed with them until I could get my place.

Well, when I finally got my place, it was in a community that was known for wealth. An area that I always dreamed of living in the community was Regent Park, a very prestigious environment. I kept asking God, "Is this really for me?" Once I settled into my new condominium, I left everyone alone for a while to reflect on my life over the last 20 years and regroup. This included my dad. I was just over the hurt that he brought to my heart over the years, mentally, physically, and emotionally.

I was still in shock that I was finally living the life l always wanted. Junior was always my biggest cheerleader and motivator in helping me accomplish my dreams and desires. He showed me that I did not have to be broke or live broke all my life. Until this day, eight years later, he always tells me, "Baby, you deserve everything that you are getting, you have been through so much and you earned all the good that's coming to you, I'm so proud of you."

After three years of living in the condominium, it forced me to either purchase it or move again. So, I decided I would finally purchase my first home. Unfortunately, those plans fell through and I had to search for a new place of residence. While searching, I was only looking for 2 bedrooms, 2 bathrooms. However, God had other plans and blessed me with a 3 bedroom, 2-1/2-bathroom town home that is all mine.

The way I came to purchase this home was with my realtor Brenda and the house was on the market when I first began my search, but it was not within my financial criteria. So, every place I looked at did not feel right. So, I had a conversation with Benita, and she said; "you will know it's your home when you walk in the door and you feel comfortable." "What you should do is write everything you want in your home, pray about it and let God do the rest." Well, that is exactly what I did, and He did the rest.

On this day, my realtor could not come with me to see the home, so she suggested I go alone, and I did. When I walked in, I felt a good vibe. I turned the corner and saw at least two of my items on the check-list then, I walked to the back of the house and over the door was the scripture that has carried me throughout my journey, "Trust in the Lord with all your heart." (Proverbs 3:5) I stopped, smiled, then cried and said, "Ok God, I hear you, you have jokes." I continued to look through-out this house, making plans on how I would design it, and then I began touching the wall and praying to repeat the address. I immediately con-tacted Brenda and told her to put an offer on the house. Now mind you, I am in the house for at least 30 minutes and I ask her when the next appointment was, and she said she was not sure.

Well, because I was not sure if I would get it, I got in the car and prayed, called Junior and told him to pray. I contacted Benita and asked her to pray and went back to my condo and told my neighbors to pray and speak the address into existence. That evening, I could not sleep and when I finally fell asleep, I dreamed about my home. I told Brenda that we would look at other places tomorrow morning and she agreed.

The next morning Brenda said, "I guess we don't need to go see the other house because you got the house." She then copied the response from the seller's agent to her and it read, "Congratulations, I meant to send this to you last night, but the seller has chosen your buyer for the home, we will begin the paperwork." I read this message several times and began to cry while thanking God. Then I paused and asked Brenda if this was real. She laughed and said, "yes, congratulations Katrina, you got the house, I'm so proud of you." For the first time after 26 years of trying to purchase a home in Philly and getting scammed out of my money, to trying in Augusta and was unsuccessful, and now after living in Charlotte for only four years, God blessed me with my first home.

LOSS, UNANSWERED QUESTIONS, HEALING,
DURING COVID-19

Globally we all had to deal with a pandemic called Coronavirus or COVID-19 exposed on March 16, 2020. During this time, so many people lost their lives or were fighting to stay alive from this devastating illness. At first, I directly did not become affected until May 30, 2020, when my dad Richard contracted the virus.

Before this time, I had stopped all communication with him, until one day, I was in Darlington at my cousin Precious's funeral services and I ran into him. I had emotions of fear and uncertainty of how he would react when he saw me. I walked up to his car and it shocked him to see me. He asked, "Boo-boo, what are you doing here?" I told him about Precious's funeral and of course, he did not have any knowledge of her dying. He said, "I'm so happy to see you, you look pretty." I said, "thank you." Then, he said, "so you didn't tell anyone you were coming home."

I said, "no, I only came for the funeral and I'm going back home." Richard said "Ol Boy" his favorite line. Then, he said, "give daddy a kiss and hug." At first, I was hesitant, but I stuck my head in the window and let him kiss me on the cheek. Then, Daddy asked if I was still in Charlotte. I said, "yes." So, he asked for my number. I went into the store to get some paper and all they had was receipt paper. Now in my mind, because of the life he lived, I figured he would lose the number or eventually it would fade, because I did not believe he would call me. Then, I left to go back home.

Unfortunately, the next time I finally saw my Dad was when my niece Julia called me in the early part of May to tell me that Daddy had his leg amputated three months ago. She figured I did not know of this and that he asked to see me. I said to her, "are you sure he asked to see me?" and she said, "yes ma'am, I don't know what happened between you and Grandpa, but he really misses you and he said that he wanted to see you." Julia said that he had changed, he was not the same Grandpa, and he would be happy to see me. So, I took a chance to visit him with my youngest daughter and my 3-month-old granddaughter, whom he had never seen. Upon arrival at the house, I saw my dad, the mover and shaker, a man who always had jokes or something crazy to say, sitting in a wheelchair looking sad and helpless.

Thinking to myself, he did not look like this when I saw him in November 2019. What happened? When he looked at me, I saw the happiness on his face; it seemed like his spirit got lifted. I kept looking at him in disbelief. That was not the daddy I knew. So, I thought, I could not confront him about the things he did to me, he probably would not remember. I told him about how much better my life had gotten and how I bought my first home and a new car. I asked if he wanted to see the car and he said yes, so I wheeled him outside so we could continue to talk.

While we were outside talking, all Daddy was doing was just staring at me. I asked him, "why are you staring at me, are you shocked that I am here. He said, "yes" and I asked him "are you proud of me and what I have done?" And he said, "yes." For a second, I felt like daddy's little girl, like this was the man I was looking for all my life since the day I met him at 21-years-old.

I told him that once he received his prosthetic leg, he could get his brother to bring him to my new home. Daddy said, "I'm going to bring myself." I laughed and we continued to talk. Over time, I had to go back home, and I still remembered Daddy asking if I was going to come back and I promised him I would. He said, "I hope you come back before it is too late." I said, "Daddy, you act like something is going to happen." He just looked at me. I hugged and kissed him and left.

For two weeks, I had my Daddy until May 28th, when he caught the coronavirus. This was the most devastating news ever. Now this virus affected me. However, I thought because my dad was often in the hospital, he would fight this. Sadly, I was wrong. The next time I saw daddy was when my siblings and I had to take him off the ventilator on July 3, 2020 and send him to hospice. Now, because I missed my sister when she passed in Hospice, as well as my aunt and cousin when they passed, I promised myself that I would be there for my dad.

On July 4, 2020, at 8:39 AM, I rang the bell at the Hospice center and announced myself to the staff and the nurse attendant said, "hold on." Out of nowhere the nurse rushes to the door and said, "come on, he just took his last breath." I said, "WHAT, NO, NO, NO." I was in a state of shock. I said, "no, he was supposed to wait until all of his kids were with him."

Endurance is Victory

Once I got in the room, he was just lying in the bed as if he was sleeping. They had removed all the tubes and machines from him. Again, I was still in disbelief, even as the nurse was confirming that he had died. They pronounced daddy deceased at 8:40 AM. I touched him and he still felt warm. I thought that these people did not know what they were talking about, he was still alive. I called my siblings to tell them to hurry to the Hospice' home.

While I was waiting for them, I was in the room with him alone and questioning why he had to leave so soon. Why I had to be the first one to be there after he took his last breath? I thought I had more time with him, to have the daddy I always wanted. And now, it was too late, I was left with so many unanswered questions, a lot of hurt and pain, and now, he would not have time to see my new chapter and how I overcame all my obstacles in life, after leaving Darryl.

At 47-years-old, I was still looking for approval from my dad. However, life changed, and I would not get that opportunity to have him to be proud of me and all that I had accomplished over the last four years.

CLOSURE WITH FAMILY AND UNDERSTANDING FOR VICTORY

Remember, earlier in my story, I told you I would explain the reason behind my nickname that I did not like. I travelled to New York to visit my uncle Brad and was talking with him about my life and childhood to get more clarification on why my family treated me so badly. So, I asked where the nickname "Muffin" come from and my aunt Felicia burst out with a hearty laugh and said, "I'm so sorry you had to go through that with your family."

Then she explained that my name came from a baby gorilla that was born in the Brooklyn Zoo the same year I was born, and the gorilla's name was "Muffin." She said she knew my Aunt Tracey was known for giving family members nicknames and she said I looked so ugly because of the skin condition that I looked like that baby gorilla and that was my nickname. I thought to myself that this family was evil. How could they treat a child this way? It was not my fault that I was born with this skin condition.

Then, I finally spoke to my mother about why she called DHS on my children all those years. She laughed and said that she was not happy that I was with Darryl, so she thought if she would call DHS on me that it would get me away from him. I thought to myself, that makes little sense at all. I told her, "do you know how much this affected your grandchildren, people coming to their schools asking those questions, and asking about them." She said it did not affect them and brushed it all off like it was not a big deal.

I also finally told my mom about what daddy did, even after Junior said he did not think I should, because I would not get the response I was looking for. And guess what, he was right. So, my mother would always ask me how daddy was before he passed, and I would say nothing. Then she said, "Oh, you must have cut him off." And I said, "yes" then she said, "well, he must have done something terrible, because you love your dad," Again, I would not say much. Then, my mom said, "you act like he touched you or something." And I could not hold it in, and I said, "yes, he tried to." The only thing my mother said, "so another man I loved, wanted you."

Endurance is Victory

By now, I was speechless, I thought, I just told you the father of your child was attempting to be inappropriate and all you can say was that, "I can't believe this." I truly thought over time she had gotten better. At that moment, I realized I had a mother and father who really did not love me, or they did not know how to show me love. But they were still my parents and I could not change that.

It took me over 30 years to have some closure with my mother's family for my healing and peace. For years, I was furious with them because I thought they knew what happened to me during my childhood and because they disliked me so much that they did not care about what happened.

But, one day, I had finally confronted some of them about how I felt, how they had treated me all those years and how they knew I was being abused and did nothing to help me. I did not expect them to be there for me during the physical abuse because some of them con- tributed to some beatings and abuse. But out of all times you need your family in your corner, was when you tell them you are being sexually abused and the most hurtful thing was that they did not help you.

So, I confronted some of my family members about how they treated me and the most shocking thing I was told was that after these years, none of them knew. Those comments and responses made me think that my Aunt Tracy never even told them about my problems considering that she was the person who was the "town gossip" and the only person who actually knew about everything from beginning to the end. After I realized this, I started asking about why they treated me so badly when I was growing up and why I was treated like an outsider by the family and out of all the cousins. To be honest, I think they never thought I would ever confront them on those issues because, in our family, they raised you to respect your elders and never question their authority.

Also, this family was excellent at keeping secrets. And because I was a kid who stuck to listening and never confronting, I would never talk back or question anything, I just did it because that was what I was told to do. But the response that I got was that they really did not understand how to treat me because they could not understand what was wrong with my skin, considering that they were young when I was born and that was something new to them.

Endurance is Victory

Believe it or not, after finally sitting down with several family members and getting a different perspective on their behavior towards me, gave me a whole new perspective for each one, especially, the other family members that I really was not close to, because I thought they were also purposely treating me badly. However, I was still not completely trustful with them because I believed people will say whatever they need to say whenever they are backed into a corner. But the only persons until this day that I will always give love to with a long handle spoon are my Aunt Tracy and my cousin Iesha because over the years, between them both, they proved to me that I was just a little pawn in their sick game of life.

Considering that I have a mother who is mentally unstable, then later on in life, meeting my father and finding that he was also mentally unstable, it has not made me hate my parents, but it has given me the spoon with a long handle of love. Because my mother has ways of making me feel guilty about anything every time she does not get her way,

I often wonder if she ever gets sick, who will be there for her. I have learned over time and I do not let it affect me in that manner because nothing will happen. I think my father had his own way of giving me the guilt trip, but he just did not know it, because I was still trying to get to know him and because I missed out on having an actual father all my life. Before I stopped communicating with him, prior to his passing, I felt as if I did do or say something wrong, he would have abandoned me, when I really needed his protection he would not have been around.

But the glorious thing about it now is that I have finally found people who are truly in my corner and I thank the Lord that He has placed these people in my life, not only for the strength but just as shoulders.

It is just sad to say that it took this long and that I had to go through all this turmoil to finally have a safety net for my children, and myself. If you have learned nothing else from this story, remember that even though life can throw you a lot of bricks and nails and it seems like you are tired of bleeding, hurting, and crying, no matter what is thrown at you, there is always something greater waiting around the corner to make it all better. Strength and perseverance will always strengthen you and give you the confidence that you can survive any-thing that comes at you in life, and in the end, you will become victo-rious.

Remember, my mother constantly put my brother's dad on this pedestal, and personally, that still affected me because I know the truth. And it was hurting me every day that they were in the dark, but I feel that because we are so close, I should be the one to tell them because my mother will never be truthful about it. Because in her eyes he was still a great man, a bishop, a faithful, and loving husband, and a noble father to her boys.

After a lot of praying and soul searching, I finally told my broth-ers what their father did to me. At first, I was nervous, but once I opened up and told them the truth, they accepted it better than I thought. My mother became very upset with me and she accused me of disrupting her home with this truth.

But that has helped me out the most, even after 30 years, I fi-nally went and got some much overdue counseling that I should have gotten at 12-years-old, because I know that I still have a lot of hurt inside of me, and I need to get it out in order for me to continue to survive. I still have a long way to go for survival, because I know I will endure a lot more pain and hurt in my life, but what I pray to God every day for is that he will always keep my children and grandchildren protected, and never allow them to go through any of the horrible things that I went through while growing up.

FINAL DESTINATION TO ENJOY MY VICTORY AND PEACE

Fast forward today, I finally own my home for the first time, something I thought throughout my life, I could never accomplish. I have better credit than I ever had since being in my home at 16-years-old. Prior to me meeting Junior, I have always lived my life with less than because of my circumstances. However, when I met Junior, my heart puller, he showed me how life is supposed to be, what I deserve as a woman who had been through so much and had so little except a good heart and a lot of hurts. During my transition to my new chapter,

I have been able to clean my credit up, and I am no longer living pay-check to pay-check.

After my divorce from Darryl, I had a negative bank account for two years where I could not pay bills but allowed all bills to come out of my account to keep everything on track, or at least I thought. With Junior being my constant cheerleader, guide, and support, I'm now paying all my bills on time and I'm not stressing about how I'm going to pay a bill and live life.

Ever since I began driving at 16 and had my vehicle, I have always had a used vehicle to drive in. But now, I have a brand-new car with all the best amenities I could ever ride in for me. I am working at the best job anyone could ever ask for, where I'm a valued team member and an asset to the company and department, and I love my job.

Endurance is Victory

So, I say to anyone who has been through what I have or worse, please know God smiles on you and shares His Grace and Mercy on His children. There will be times when you feel like giving up, thinking you are not worthy of better or you will not see the sunshine at the end of the tunnel. Trust me, you will see the brightest of the sunlight that will shine directly on you. But as I always say to people who see me and say, "you're always so happy and bubbly" and my response will always be, "If you only knew my story, you would understand my smile."

With Love, Morgan Rees

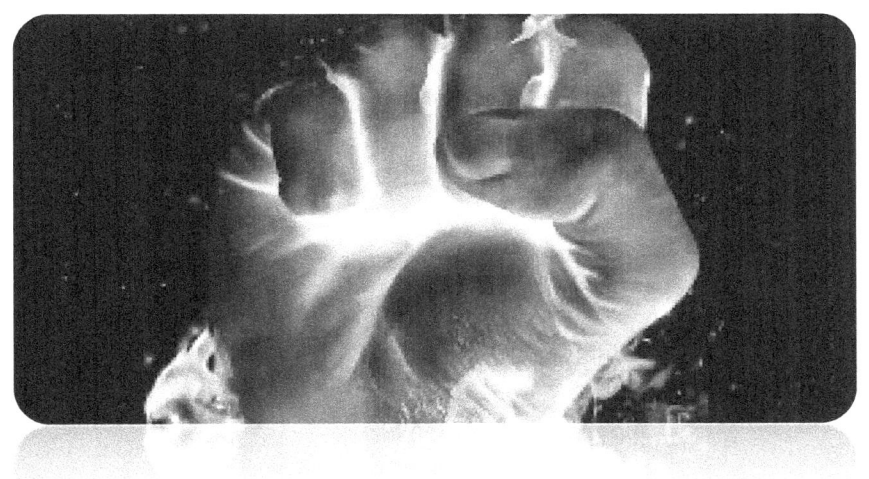

Trust in the LORD with all your HEART…

Proverb 3:5

Endurance is Victory